A DYING GENERATION

WILLIAM LINCOLN

Copyright © 2017 William Lincoln

All rights reserved.

ISBN: 9781520468570

TABLE OF CONTENTS

GOOD MORNING. 22
THE PEOPLE 31
MY REALITY WILL BRING AWARENESS TO PROBLEMS IN OUR COMMUNITIES. 67
THE "N" WORD 126
THOUGHTS ON TODAY PARENTHOOD 133
A MESSAGE FOR THE QUEENS 150
A MESSAGE FOR THE KINGS 199
REFLECTIONS 229
SUPPORTING 253
    NEECEE SIMMONS 254
    STACEY BLACK 259
    JEREMY "DJ MIX-I-AM" REAVES 265
    DOMINIC R WILLIAMS 267
    MICHAEL M. WILLIAMS 269
    VERONICA PEARSON 271
    JAMILA GREEN 277
    SPECIAL REYNOLDS 279
    JUAN SAMUEL 287
    JON BRICK 305
    ARMINTA MCKINNEY 307

At a young age I was faced with adversity; I had to overcome being homeless, being a parent at 17, gang activity, and the story goes on. After seeing most of my friends die in the streets or get locked up, I decided a change needed to happen. My conscious spoke to me and reminded me that I was better than the situation I was in. To change required pushing myself to do better, so I joined the United States Navy and served 11 years. Then, I got my Bachelor of Science degree in Business from Phoenix University. I am an author and I am also apart of Phi Beta Sigma, a Fraternity that focuses on helping the community.

Currently I share my life experiences and travel to different communities, streets, and churches to speak with and uplift our youth. My mission is to help them in any way I can and to motivate them to become the best people they can be. It is my belief that when a person becomes successful you do not leave your community, but you come back and make an impact. This is a guaranteed way that we can make a difference and start a new positive legacy for others to continue when they become successful.

By the Grace of God, I made it out. Now it is time

to go back and get others! This Generation needs us more than ever and it is time for us to answer the call. I have asked people one simple question: What do you think about today's Generation, Culture, and/or Society? I wanted to hear from the people because I am trying to better understand where our community stands. I have asked these questions to see if we have accurately described the problem and have the resources to find answers for them. I have received different views from people with different backgrounds. My main concerns are dealing with my community which is the African American community. Push them to do better so the future will be brighter for our children.

I am a firm believer that no matter our Race, Ethnicity, or Background we all should come together as ONE. Judge a man by the content of their character and not by the color of his skin. I believe we forget those powerful words spoken by Dr. Martin Luther King Jr. The hate against Blacks and Blacks hating on other Blacks due to darker or lighter skin, backgrounds, neighborhoods, and so many other different hate reasons needs to stop.

The killing of young boys and raping of women,

needs to stop in our communities. The gang violence needs to stop. Parents not wanting to be parents needs to stop. Fathers being absent need to stop. Not having knowledge on your finances needs to stop. Growing counts of homeless teens need to stop. Being killed by the Police. . . Needs to Stop. . .

This book was written to help start the conversation around how to do better and help others. Also, knowing who you are and where you come from helps with identity. For those who may not know who they truly are or their history. That is where the African proverbs come into play. I pray to God that this book helps to save someone's life or help change someone's life for the better. Thank you for taking time to read this. I ask you with everything that is going on in this WORLD: What do you think about today's Generation, Culture, and Society?

You are full of Greatness no matter your background or situation you are dealing with. . . You must believe in yourself. . . You must believe in God… Stop being afraid to go after your Purpose. . . Go after your Greatness. . . It does not matter if you have a criminal background, grew up in poverty, suffer any type of abuse, homeless or grew up in foster care, and so on. . . YOU HAVE A PURPOSE AND YOU ARE FULL OF GREATNESS. . . IT IS UP TO YOU TO BELIEVE IN YOU. . . Because everyone may not believe in you, so it is important that you BELIEVE in yourself. . . That is the fuel that will keep you going regardless of what others may say. . .

This book is dedicated to

Laquez Lincoln

The last thing you said to me was you want to be just like me. So that made me transform into a man that I would want you to look up to. Because of your words I have become a better man. I will never forget those words little cuz. I keep it in my everyday life. . . I thank you for those words. . . I thank God for you. . . Hoping To Make You Proud

Love You Always and Forever Miss You. . .

Your Big Cuz,

William

WILLIAM LINCOLN

I AM BECAUSE YOU ARE
AFRICAN PROVERBS

Art by: Jon Brick (BrickArt)

jonbrickart@gmail.com

I WOULD LIKE TO THANK GOD, FAMILY, AND FRIENDS WHO HELP PUT THIS TOGETHER...

WILLIAM LINCOLN

Wisdom is Wealth
Swahili Proverbs

If you think you are too small to make a difference, you haven't spent the night with a mosquito.

African Proverbs

WILLIAM LINCOLN

This Generation Needs

LOVE

To show that someone actually care

WILLIAM LINCOLN

GUIDANCE

To show them the right PATH

CONSISTANCY

To show you are always there

COMMITMENT
To show they can depend on you

PRAYER

To keep them protected

You are full of Greatness no matter the background you have or situation you are dealing with. . . You must believe in yourself. . . You must believe in God. . . Stop being afraid to go after your Purpose. . . Go after your Greatness. . . It doesn't matter if you have a criminal background, grew up in poverty, suffer any type of abuse, homeless or grew up in foster care, and so on. . . YOU HAVE A PURPOSE AND YOU ARE FULL OF GREATNESS. . . IT'S UP TO YOU TO BELIEVE IN YOU. . . Because everyone may not believe in you so it's important that you Believe in yourself. . . That's the fuel that will keep you going regardless of what others may say. . .

***

A DYING GENERATION

Good Morning.

. .

Two words that we take for granted. Just to be able to say those words to someone else and not realizing others wish they had another chance to be able to say those same words. Good Morning defines a new day, a new chance, a new opportunity, and a new way of life that can begin today. Good Night defines the end of the day and also for some the end of Life. I am trying to give the opportunity for more young people of color the ability to say Good Morning. I am watching too many young people all over dying like they do not have the option to live, walking over too many blood stains on concrete, and scrolling down timelines seeing too many R.I.Ps. Tomorrow is never promised. So let's start teaching our culture the importance of Good Morning...

Good Morning Everyone...

Black lives matter was not created to void out the lives of other ethnic groups. Black lives matter was created to inform our culture that each and every African American life is worth living. It is not to be racist or support hatred. We are tired of seeing our culture slowly dying in front of our face. We are tired of seeing Blacks on the news involved in police brutality and Black people killing each other off.

We are tired of seeing our children dying on the streets and others going to jail day after day. We are tired of our culture living in mental slavery thinking that the street life is the only life. If your culture was in the same condition as ours, I would expect for you to do something about it.

It can be very challenging walking this earth with darker skin and dealing with the discrimination, racism, prejudice, and those who have slavery based mind frames and think that being Black is being wrong. If you are not Black then it will be hard for you to understand as if I was White to understand some of the problems White people deal with.

We all have struggles but I refuse to let my culture

die in front of my face. My children have to live in this world and I will make it my business to make their generation and culture greater or I will die trying.

Welcome and thank you for joining this important journey where we are trying to uplift and encourage our communities. As we all know there is a War against the Black community by the System and even War against each other. There have been too many unnecessary funerals one after another. There has been too many Candle Light Vigils we have attended. Souls are being lost, Innocents lives are being taken, and Freedom is being capture and locked down. So once again I thank you for helping us to save

A DYING GENERATION

What do you think about today's Generation, Culture, and/or Society? I wanted to hear from the people because I am trying to understand where our community stands. I have asked these questions to see if we described the problem and find answers for them. I have heard different views from people with different backgrounds. My main concerns are dealing with my community which is the Black community. Push them to do better so the future will be brighter for our children.

I am a firm believer that no matter our Race, Ethnicity, or Background we all should come together as ONE. Judge a man by the content of character and not by the color of his skin. I believe we forget those powerful words spoken by Dr. Martin Luther King Jr. The hate against Blacks and Blacks hating on other Blacks due to darker or lighter skin, back ground, neighborhoods, and so many other different hate reasons need to stop.

The killing of young boys and raping of young ladies, needs to stop in our communities. The gang violence needs to stop. Parents not wanting to be parents needs to stop. The absence of Fathers needs to stop. Not having knowledge on your finances needs to stop. Growing counts of homeless teens needs to stop. Being killed by the Police. . . Needs To Stop. . .

***

So I ask you with everything that is going on in this WORLD: What do you think about today's Generation, Culture, and/or Society?

When there is no enemy within,

the enemies outside cannot hurt you.

African proverb

A DYING GENERATION

This piece is by a very special person. She is my niece Ms. Dione Smith who is a great young lady with a powerful future ahead of her. She is a young lady with a wise soul. She is an award winning poet whom I consider "The Voice Of The Young People". This is the poem that she wrote to win a poetry contest. This is a poem that I believe everyone needs to read. It was written about her Father. You might want to not only read but also listen to the words. Her father inspired her to write this piece called "I Still Want To".

We encourage all Black Men to start stepping up in all areas. A Strong Black Man is becoming a dying breed that we must save. Too many children have been let down and too many mothers have been left alone to do all the hard work. We cannot expect change unless we change.

I know so many people, friends, and family that grew up without a father. Sometimes you expect for people to say my Father was not there or I don't have a relationship with him. This must change now.

A DYING GENERATION

By: Dione Smith

I still wanted to say that I have the best dad… A great dad… The they wish I had Kind of dad… Not even mad at my dad… Even though he made me… Feel bad, feel sad, feel like I wish I never had… I still wanted to, but now I can't…

I don't want to even see you… Be near you… Claim you were the dear you… When now you're not you… You're the selfish down right hell- wished you apparently something was broken battered into… Well did you know I still wanted to… And yet you…

You left your Family, No our Family, shattered battered in two… You would think we as a Society would be sick of the whole dead beat dad scene and yet you run around and mock and downsize the word "WE"…

But Father for you

I wanted you to Know

I still wanted to…

***

The People

Read as the People Voice Their Experiences, Opinions, and Feelings about Today's Society and Generation……..

A DYING GENERATION

A lost generation.

I grew up in the seventies. I was a product of the civil rights era; The James Brown, I'm Black and I'm proud movement and the mantra of Malcolm X and Marcus Garvey. We were politically and socially aware of self, our rich history, culture, legacy and self-worth. I grew up during an era when you feared AND respected your parents and elders and held them in high esteem. I grew up in an era when it was mandatory to attend school and get an education and aspire to do better than your parents. I grew up at a time when doing household chores were the norm and your responsibility. I grew up in an era where the church was a respected institution. I grew up at a time where life and property were highly valued. The seventies may not have been the best decade but it was far from being the worse as the worse was just around the corner.

Fast forward to current times and sadly I don't recognize the generations that have come after me. Where did we go wrong, what happened, how did we take a wrong turn from I'm Black and I'm Proud to the misogynists of bitches and hoes as the cultural norms. As I attempt to examine how we got here, one way to understand the "lost generation" is to view segments of the highly acclaimed HBO series *The Wire*, a show that took a realistic sociological and political look of life in the urban city of Baltimore which sadly could be attributed to any urban city in America. This show shows an accurate portrayal and reveals a lot about the lost generation.

As I attempt to dig deep into the root of the emergence of this lost generation, it is my opinion that it was the introduction and eventual pandemic of crack-cocaine which largely aided in the disintegration of the Black family and setting the stage for despair and hopelessness for the future generation. In my opinion, the mass influx and pandemic of crack in the Black community had a significant NEGATIVE cause and effect on the lost generation. Crack created a culture of crack addicted parents and crack babies.

Often times parents, both mothers and fathers and sometimes entire families were addicted which eventually cause them to lose their homes, livelihood, self-worth and more importantly their children ended up being collaterals. Crack addicted parents would often spend their days and nights high on drugs 24/7 and neglected to raise and take care of their children responsibly. As a result children at a very young age were often left to raise and fend for themselves and their younger siblings as entire families became broken and separated. This often times left children homeless with nowhere to go but in the foster care or juvenile system or to live on the streets.

If I ask the question, what or who is to be blamed for the lost generation, I blame the drug *Crack* as one of the major influences, in a variety of ways it left young children without the love, support and guidance of responsible parents or guardians at a very critical stage of their lives. Many children were abandoned and left without structure and positive influences in their lives. As a result of this cycle, many dropped out of school during their formative years as they had no one to take them or encourage them to go to school and get an education.

Education became the least of their priorities and was replaced with the struggles of surviving life in the system or on the streets. For those who ended up on the streets, the streets became their institution and learning ground; the streets became their school and their church. Kids were now being raised by the streets and began to become products of the streets, swearing by the street code of kill or be killed as the Ethos of Survival. Not only did they start to run the streets, but the streets started to run them and within time became their primal guide to a path of self-hate, desperation, despair, and self-destruction. The streets became their university, their playground, their home, their educators, and their family. The young and abandoned made the street their refuge and the drug dealers, pushers, pimps, and prostitutes replaced the safety and stability of the home and family; and became their parents and teachers. But instead of being educated and being made aware of their past greatness, history and legacy, they were exploited sexually, physically and emotionally and this became the cycle of their existence. The church that was once revered and respected as part of the village were missing and children were left without any parental figure or mentors to guide, nurture, teach, and discipline them in their childhood and young upbringing. Unfortunately, this part of their life cycle completely disappeared and no longer existed for them. Many never even experienced anything but growing up on the streets and took on the harsh street culture.

As a result of this parental and familial abandonment, street exploitation and destructive cycle, these children became lost and began to live their lives fearlessly and with no regards for self or any other life. Many became, selfish, ruthless and self-centered. This lost generation grew up without parents, families, teachers or mentors to show them responsible and positive behaviors and foster the development of self-worth. These children became lost because they also lacked education and significant positive influences.

The only thing that mattered to them was surviving on the streets and their current status on the corner. As a result, many boys grew up to be like their street idols-the pimps and drug dealers as that was all they saw and knew, likewise many girls grew up lacking self-worth and pride and did what they needed to survive because that was all they saw and knew. Within a few short decades, the reality of a lost generation emerged.

The lost generation is attributed to a legacy of abandoned children and children raising children; A legacy of lack of self-worth and self-love. As a result of this cycle, they bore children and repeated the cycle of addictions and abandonment as they had no examples of what was right. Now we see the current generation with little or no respect for themselves or others including their elders, and the continual lack of education and the kill or be killed mentality.

I am not concluding that *Crack* is solely responsible for the lost/dying generation, but in several ways it aided and exacerbated it and I would love to know how this generation would have fared and transformed had *Crack* not came on the scene. The "it takes a village" sentiments disappeared and what we now see is a different set of principles and mindsets which stemmed from being raised without parents, discipline and guidance but the harshness of living on the streets. Many are illiterate and have no basic education, life and coping skills. Babies are regularly having babies and grandparents are now in their 30s and many take pride in that.

You can't teach something you don't know and everything is a learned behavior. It is my ultimate hope the lost generation will one day find their way back to greatness.

KN Williams

Author, Speaker and Youth Advocate

While attending Thomas Jefferson High School in Brooklyn, New York, I lived in constant fear that I would be a victim of a school shooting. During my sophomore year I experienced gun violence first hand. On November 16, 1991, Robert D. McFadden of the New York Times reported that A youth trying to help his brother in a fistfight drew a gun and opened fire in the crowded hallway of a Brooklyn high school yesterday, and the wild shots killed a 16-year-old student bystander and critically wounded a teacher who was approaching to intervene. After firing three shots with a 9-millimeter automatic, the young gunman escaped as the victims staggered and fell and screams and confusion engulfed the third floor hallway at Thomas Jefferson High School at 400 Pennsylvania Avenue in the East New York section shortly before 10:30 A.M. Less than two months later, Thomas Jefferson High School and the East New York community would be rocked by another school shooting. On the same day as New York City Mayor David M. Dinkins visit, two students were shot dead just in the hall way just hours before Mayor Dinkins was to give a speech on empowerment and avoiding the pitfalls of drugs and alcohol.

A DYING GENERATION

New York Times reporter Alison Mitchell wrote that The brazen killing at Thomas Jefferson High School took place just 15 feet away from two police officers who were part of the school's normal security detail, the police said. Thirteen security guards were also in the school, and an additional 10 police officers were assigned outside for the Mayor's visit. A Jefferson student pulled out a .38-caliber pistol and without a word shot 17-year-old Ian Moore once in the chest and 16-year-old Tyrone Sinkler once in the back of the head, on the second floor of the high school, the police said. He ran out a back door, with school security guards in pursuit, and was caught two blocks away. The police identified the suspect as Khalil Sumpter, 15 years old. "I'm standing there," said Lewis Tanner, 19, who was in the hallway near the shooting. "I had my head down. I heard shots and I ran." He said other students were also running and crying. "I didn't see what happened because I ran," he said. "Thank God I got away. They weren't looking for me." Third Youth Shot in Head Attending Thomas Jefferson High School during the early 1990s felt like I was attending school in a war zone.

I lived in constant fear that there would be yet another shooting and my friends or even I would fall victim to senseless violence. I realized that the only way to persevere through this cycle of violence was to continue to be a great student, graduate on time, and attend college. I choose to remain a student at Thomas Jefferson High School because I believed that to transfer to a different high school would just be an easy way out. In June of 1994 I graduated with an 83 average and was accepted to Syracuse University where I majored in Political Science.

Dr. Billie Dee Tate

A DYING GENERATION

1987: I was a rebellious eighth grader who spent more time in the principal's office than in class. I had discovered punk rock when I was eleven years old, but was now discovering my role in the scene. Loud, fast music screaming obscenities; ripped jeans and t-shirts held together with safety pins, and a penchant for fighting, drinking, hitting on girls, and refusing to work.

They all had their reasons: the fighting because of the countless "faggot" comments I got from the athletes, rednecks, and preppies every day for the way I dressed, the drinking because my family was falling apart at the seams, the hitting on girls because of the cocktail of hormones puberty was dealing me, and the refusing to work because I was straight up lazy. All of which, in some form or another, landed me in that hard wooden chair in front of a fat oak principal's desk that was only slightly wider than the woman who occupied it. A wooden yard stick leaned against a file cabinet of "permanent records" as a reminder of better times when she could use it to flog a student without fearing a law suit.

"I have called your parents," she told me one time in the office. That day, I had suffered two offenses.

1- Not doing my homework and 2- fighting during recess with some bully. The first, plain and simple happened the way it sounded; I did not do the work. The second, however, ended with the bully whining to a teacher all swollen-eyed and glass-jawed because he had never had one of his prospective victims punch him in the face . . . especially not in front of all the girls he was trying to impress.

Regardless of my street toughness, those words I have called your parents sat in his gut like ten pounds of clay.

Before my parents arrived, the principal said, "You COULD be anything you want, why do you choose this?" She gesticulated to my wardrobe as a whole with a dismissive, fluttering hand, but I knew she meant my unruly attitude as well.

When my parents arrived, the principal simply stated that we would talk in the conference room down the hall.

I caught the eye of my father, whose mouth was turned down into a scowl like a bulldog ready to crush a cat between his teeth. My mother's look was not as aggressive but every bit as wounding because it reflected frustrated disappointment. Individually, I had learned to deal with either one, but they were rarely in unison on something as they were that day.

In the conference room, the principal sat on one side of the conference table, and I sat on the other, anticipating the cold chill of my parent's book-ending me. Instead, they sat right next to the principal, staring down at me like that table was the scope of a gun.

"What did you do?" my father asked disgusted.

Today years later, I am an educator, while many of my punk rock friends and accomplices in high school are prisoners, junkies, and corpses.

And some of these friends had the coolest parents in the world, too!

They let their kids drink and even smoke POT at home. Unfiltered, they talked about everything with their kids; including how hard they used to party and how many people they had sex with when they were their kids' age. Great, right? My mom, my dad, my best friends.

Not at all . . .

... Especially not on the teacher's side of the table hearing how a child does not lie, manipulate, bully, or deceive.

Johnny wouldn't do that . . . Ebony doesn't do that at home . . . He says you never assigned it.

The meeting has become all too common and twofold. The first is addressing the issue with the child, and the second is having an intervention where I try to convince someone in complete denial that his/her child is not perfect (and not in that order). Best case scenario, a resolution that favors the child emerges; and worst case scenario, they get disgruntled and report me to someone above me who will side with the parents and demand that I resolve the issue in the child's favor. I begin to question myself. Am I in the wrong and being unfair?

When I ask the student's other teachers, I get, "Yeah, s/he is failing my class too and acts like a total asshole. . . "yes, educators talk like that . . . "but you know they're not going to do anything about it." They, in this case, could be referring to either the parents or the administrators.

So where does that get me?

If I'm bold enough to push the issue, I will end up at the conference table sitting alone on one side facing parents and an administrator on the other side. The parents scowl at me like bulldogs while the administrator stares at me in frustration and disappointment. The only thing that has changed since I was a teen is the addition of a student maintaining a facade of humility. S/he sits with impunity, smiling behind sullen eyes understanding the clear message being given.

"You SHOULD be anything you want."

The student leaves the table to get ice cream with mom and/or dad just like they would with their other friends. They complain a bit more about me, and Mom and Dad agree like Stepford parents. When she gets home, Mom sends me the following email:

Thank you for taking time to speak with us. I will be sure that XXXXX will get that assignment to you. I assure you that he did not know it was due two weeks ago. Perhaps in the future you should make sure that each student understands how to do every assignment and when it is supposed to be turned in. I want to be sure that XXXXX does well in you class, so what can you do to help him in class?

I think:

Everyone else in class turned in the assignment on time. The assignment had been on the board since the first day of class and I checked each child's notebook to make sure it was in there. As far as what I can do to help YOUR child? I can suggest that YOU look at his grades every week on the website, that YOU check his assignment book every night, and that YOU realize that he is your child, not your buddy, and I am an educator with no motivation to lie, call you at home, or arrange a meeting superfluously. Your child is a disruption in class and should be failing if only modern practices in education would allow me to do so. If you do not start setting standards, teaching how to avoid failure, and enforcing accountability, then you are looking at a future of far more problems than missing a homework assignment.

Dr. Brett Butler

A Group of Educators Collectively Had This To Say

Today's educational system does a disservice to our youth in urban communities. The school that I work out is systematically preparing them for jail (having them walk on the painted blue line, hands at their sides), lack of social abilities (can't talk during lunch-there's no scheduled recess for grades 3-6).

We are teaching to the test. The students do not learn other necessary attributes. The majority of my 4th grade students read at a 1st grade level, AR (accelerated reading) wasn't a priority, now it is when the students are not accustomed to reading daily; and most of their parents can't read.

Homework is no longer a requirement because home life has changed dramatically. Most students go home to no one or someone who is inept; therefore it's not benefitting the student. The students are capable of far greater than they are being credited for. I believe in every single one of my students, and I pray that they start to believe in themselves.

Sharon (Teacher)

Our education system is numbers driven. It needs to be more community based. Too many folks running out of the classroom but still in education.

JoeAnn (Teacher)

All schools should and must be afforded the same money, new buildings, updated materials, supplies and good staff. The best schools are not just for the elite students; all our students must have the same opportunities.

I love magnet schools don't get it twisted; because they are doing what the other schools should be able to do but are deprived of the resources;

Strict, discipline, parental involvement a must, and teacher and student accountability.

No tolerance for disrespect or your child is out the door. So why don't we demand this same expectation from schools that are not magnet schools. If your kid cannot and will not conform to the rules they need to sit out a year with their parents.

I think they are doing a good job with what they

have to work with. If only more money was allocated towards education, total education. The system would be excellent. Board members that consist of teachers, parents, business people, clergy, and students should make crucial decisions for our schools. And accountability from all groups listed above. We must work together listening to all sides before making a decision. The money in the school system must be allocated to all schools not just magnet schools.

I feel us as a culture the time is now to rebuild a healthy and wealthy nation! I believe we have to step up and stop living in the slavery of our own minds and stop allowing the corporation of America to rape our humanity, our sanity, and Our Heritage! We As A Strong Community Have To Stand Together And Transform The Minds Of Our Youth With The Truth Of Life So They Can Build in Love and Not In Fear! Bridging the Gaps of Our Communities. My Is Our HLVII/CJE Movement We Doing Here In Baltimore.

Nikita Chase

REECE C.

Titled: An Open Letter

We have a generation that is dying off due to so many challenges that face them day to day. Dear young people, where have we wronged you? Why are you killing each other? Why are you so angry? The many generations before you have let you down, we have allowed the ball to drop in society, our communities, and in the homes today. We no longer take the time to listen and understand your pain and frustration, instead we assume you can handle what life throws at you but we do not provide the guidance that is needed to survive in this world. Please understand that we are all in this fight together, no more will you stand alone. No more will you go through life without a shoulder to lean on or someone to be your voice when trials and tribulations have kept you silent.

It is time to come together and fight this war on gun violence, poverty, loss of education, and misguidance for these new generations and the many to follow. Although it can seem hard to trust, don't ever stop believing in God because he has never given up on you or your situation. Don't lose faith in people, there are some who will and have made a difference in this world today and it's something to always be proud about.

Now. . .will you continue to help in aiding the problems today or will you rise up, stand tall and fight this battle with us?

ALWAYS HAS BEEN YOUR CHOICE. . .

Our society is plagued by so many of our children believing social media is life and that putting stuff on social media really makes people truly like them or love them. But they are not understanding once it's out there you can't take it back. Twerking, sexual acts, and fighting are at the top of the list of things they are doing... Our children have to know their worth Even though we as Adults sometimes don't even know. . .

Adrienne Williams

Quick to build schools with the most up to date technology outside of this country, but still we have schools right here in our own backyards that are suffering! The youth in cities across the U.S. are suffering. . . #staywoke

Chris Coward

How do I feel about society today as a whole? Honestly I'm numb with license should I see now I've got used to it. This generation is lost and they're just trying to find their way. It's not like it was awesome growing up in the nineties we have a little more respect for those who are older than us. This generation just doesn't care at all I feel like society doesn't care at all. It's all about the almighty dollar

LaQuenton Jones

Dying generation is so factual and true there is no other way to categorize this lost generation. However, the bible speaks diligently of things that are occurring and will occur. I feel like we are living in a confused, lost and self-absorb generation. This generation is dying because it lacks structure, spirituality, unity and positive upbringings. Males are slacking with the duties of a father; mothers are single aiming to deliver something a woman can never do totally alone. I can continue to go on and on. But the answer to this question is I feel this generation is completely lost of structure. I hope this help please keep me posted.

Nisha Mitchell

Interview with Grant Whitesell

Me: What are your thoughts of today's generation?

Grant Whitesell: You mean like young people? 'Millennials?'

Me: yes sir

Grant Whitesell: They are the group I worry about the least. They don't buy into old prejudices and backwards ways of thinking that are second nature to the older generations.

Me: Which group do you worry about the most and why

Grant Whitesell: Honestly? Angry, bitter, greedy, old White men in positions of power and privilege. I also worry about the working-class White people they've fooled into supporting them against their own best interests.

Grant Whitesell

One of my greatest problems is seeing those who have, watching those who don't suffer. Even family, they are so unapologetic and try to cover up and convince themselves that they are "lazy". In reality, you are to help the fellow man. It's an unwritten law. For example, I live in a city much smaller than New York City. But all we hear about is meth and pill busts. It's an epidemic here. The addiction feeds off of a lack of opportunity and a feeling of hopelessness. These people are not lazy, they need help. They went to these drugs because they want nothing to do with life. Meanwhile the rich and even middle class walk around in their own swamp of dirt and grime. Clean the community and help one another and smile. This is what's wrong in my society.

Greg Russell

This Generation is in need of understanding, modeling, coaching, and to be educated in all aspects of life.

Thomas Davis

This generation is just a culmination of bad choices made by the previous two generations that preceded them. They are the kids of generation X and this is what happens when you spare the rod and make your child your friend and your peer instead of being their parents. Their parents dropped the ball and let the television raise them instead of the parents doing their jobs. Hence, this is why these kids are overtly entitled and narcissistic.

Juan Rich

First of all, I would like to thank William Lincoln for allowing me to write something in this book of his. God is working through him and this book is the result. My thoughts are of this next generation. I sincerely hope that there is room in their lives for the presence of God to flourish. If there is not room, please make room. It's too easy to go on and create situations around you that look manageable, but are not. The world would have you believe that anything that is in the Bible is outdated and not worth reading and understanding. It is the story of our heritage, and the world you know would have you believe it's all a myth. When documentation exists that tells you that you are related to these characters in the scriptures, and that there is hope for you as old as the very earth we walk on every day, that's when your life opens up. Yes, Black lives matter! They matter because they are the beginning of other lives that also matter. Please know that in all your getting, remember who you are. The blood of Kings and Queens runs through your veins, not by myth, but in reality. Please remember God is your resource, your strength, your Rock. Whatever this world tells you about yourself, YOU ARE GODS CHILDREN. Nothing can separate you from God's love, not even you, God's greatest creation! May God bless you, and may His face shine upon you and give you Peace!

Rev. Stephen E. Benson

With everything going on in the Black community, I really feel that we need to go back to community childrearing. I am a firm believer of the saying "it takes a village to raise a child". Having a network of people to help build strong children is vital. We need more fathers and mentors to commit to the upbringing of our young men. We need strong women to teach our young girls how to uplift each other instead of tearing each other down.

Shavonne Black

As a society, we are all in deep trouble. All of society has been brainwashed in one way or another ... From racism all the way across the spectrum to accept the poison in the foods we are eating. The 1% that controls this entire world is hiding many truths from society. Societies only hope is to lean on the few who are in search of these truths. I personally have hope because we live in the information age and I see more and more people waking up.

Grady McCain

What you learn is what you die with.
~African Proverbs

An army of sheep led by a lion can defeat an army of lions led by a sheep.
~ Ghanaian proverb

***

WILLIAM LINCOLN

My Reality Will Bring Awareness to Problems in Our Communities…

Control the people with fear and the people will look for a savior. Release a Nightmare to give them a new fear and do away with hope now we have their attention. Because now, the people look for us to save them.

Government vs. The People

This environment got us acting violent and the government makes more money when there's no culture alliance. They don't want us to find out who's lying and become defiant and dissect their laws of science,

And now they're scared that I may bring people together and build a covenant, That's why the government call themselves Big Brother and wants to destroy Africa the Motherland and leaves us Motherless, But knowing we ready to go home so they hide the Mother ship,

But then again, as I look Back, My ancestors built America on their Backs, I plan to own what my family helped Built, So I want what's owed to us so tell King Leopold II of Belgium since we lend him a hand it's time to payback.

In the past they put chains around your legs and today they put chains around your thinking, genocide each other with over 700 homicides in Chicago and over 2 million children homeless in America it's time to answer the call their hopeless screams is the sound of the phone ringing

No President, congressman, or any government elect can fix our community especially when we can and need to fix it ourselves, what's the use of the oppress asking the oppressors for HELP

MY REALITY

So today like any other day I walked to the metro which is like a mile from my home. You seem to always see something that reflects on today's society or your reality. Earlier I saw and helped a man that was just lying on the ground at a gas station on the corner of Suitland and Silver Hill Rd. To be honest I wasn't going to help and just walk pass him like everyone else. He was across the street from where I was walking.

But God made me feel conviction and I had to go back. Not only did I go back but called the police & ambulance and waited with him. They came and said he was freezing. Which h means of course he had been outside for a while. That part didn't bother me. It was the fact that in the morning that intersection is super busy. What got me was when I started thinking of how many people just walked or drove by without a care in the world because to us it's the norm. We are talking about a man that was lying on the ground up North in the middle of January. Nobody felt that it was their concern.

That has to change. The same morning, I seen a young girl with maybe a jacket on; cold with her new baby covered in a blanket waiting for the train to come. I wonder where your family, child's father, or support is. I wanted to give her my coat. A change has to come someday . . . .**But every day I see things that still remind me that we have a long way to go. . .**

Life Lessons

Too many of our young Black men are committing accidental suicide in this war called LIFE. The lessons that were taught or were not taught are making funeral homes richer by the day. They fall into traps such as being accepted by others and not accepting themselves. Being shown that street life is the only life they can live. We must show them there is much more to life than the streets. Show them it's okay to be different and they have a choice not to live by the gun.

Help your child to not be a product of his or her own environment. Take them out the box even if it's just a day on the bus. Take them somewhere that looks different than what they know so they can have in the back of their minds a choice that there is a bigger world outside the hood. The streets have a way of teaching our youth about life. Make sure you teach them first.

God Was My Last Choice Not First

I'm not perfect. . I've done a lot of things in my past. . . I have regrets . . . There are things I'm still battling today. . . There was a time I was depressed and felt like I didn't need anyone help. . . I fooled myself believing that I could really go through life without anyone's help. . . God was not my first Choice to call on for help. . . Even when I felt that I could save these young people from dying. . . But now I ask him to help me to help them. . . They need God and they need US. . . Use your mistakes and regrets as knowledge and wisdom to help younger people from making the same mistakes. . . Let's start teaching them about God. . . The God who helped you defeat your drug habit. . . The God who helped you defeat your drinking problem . . . The God who helped you live after getting shot from being in the streets . . . The God who helped your marriage. . . The God who helped you defeat your gambling problem. . . The God who helped you get through prison time… The God who set you free. . . The God who helped you become a present and not absent father. . . The God who helped you overcome depression. . . The God who helped you overcome your suicide thoughts… The God who helped you PERIOD. . . We need him because we cannot do it alone. . .

Stop Holding Each Other Back

We seem to be the only race that continues to hold each other back from reaching the promise land. Selfishness and Ignorance continue to spread like an epidemic disease. We don't want someone else to make it just because we don't have our priorities in order. So because we don't have our priorities in order you cannot shine or surpass me. Jealousy is an ugly character that can suppress your own future.

So because we don't want anyone to surpass us we continue to bring others down when they are close to reaching their goals and dreams. Or better yet we will even try to diminish other dreams when they try to form the thought of dreaming. When will we stop being crabs and become the person that holds the ladder steady to help the next person or generation climb to their dreams. Understand the power of your words holds the power of Life and Death.

Actions Creates Judging

It's a damn shame I must watch my back every day. It's sad that for me just to take a jog in the morning it must be a critical thought process just because of my skin color. A Black man in a hoodie running while night is a picture painted that reflects negative attention. Prejudge before actions shows I'm just running.

There are some things in my life that should be an easy answer is more of critical equation to figure out just because the color of my skin. Equality does not always come often. For me knowing this I must make every decision as if my life depends on it. I must not put myself in any situation that will allow me to be judged by the law of the land. I must understand that if the system was not made for me then why I would give the system a chance to enslave me. I met many brothers and sisters who know the system, understand the system, and still put themselves in the system. Then you have those who don't know so we must educate ourselves. Let's do better as a whole and educate on why we don't belong in the system and also the reason behind the system.

According to a Wonkblog analysis of government statistics, about 1.6 percent of prime-age White men (25 to 54 years old) are institutionalized. If all those 590,000 people were recognized as unemployed, the unemployment rate for prime-age White men would increase from about 5 percent to 6.4 percent.

For prime-age Black men, though, the unemployment rate would jump from 11 percent to 19 percent. That's because a far higher fraction of Black men — 7.7 percent, or 580,000 people — are institutionalized.

It's A Problem When You Are Ashamed of God

God. . . A word that some of us slide a way from just to try to fit in today society. It's funny when things are going good you hardly hear God's name being praise or rejoiced. But when the storm comes and trouble starts knocking on your door we are quick to fall on the floor, raise our hands, and raise his name. Nobody is invincible especially when you are going by your own actions. You start a cycle that transforms into a system that you live by.

That's why you continue to do the same things, get into the same trouble, deal with the same type of people, dealing with the same type of hurt, feeling the same type of emptiness, feeling the same type of confuse, and etc. There is nothing else to say. Rather you are going to accept him or you are not. Rather you are going to be proud of knowing and accept his Love or you are not.

Black People Hating On Other Black People Because of Skin Color

Why do you hate your brother? Why do you hate your sister? We are fighting the same fight and yet you still don't understand what those have been trying to teach us who came before us. United We Stand. . . Divided We Fall. . . At the end when one dies we all lose. . . If we can come together as one, then maybe we will have a future instead of killing and bringing each other down as individuals.

We continue to hate on others because of their different shade of black. Maybe it came from slavery when lighter colored Blacks worked in the house and the darker colored Blacks worked in the field. All I do know was that slaves were being raped, hurt, and killed. THEY ALL WERE STILL SLAVES REGARDLESS OF THEIR SHADE OF BLACK.

It shouldn't matter if someone is light skin, brown skin, or has a darker complexation. We should still love each other. We are all still fighting the same fight. Death or Jail is not racists or prejudices. Learn To Love One Another And Not Hate One Another. . .

Judge With No Purpose

What do you see when you look at me?

You judge me without knowing me

See my pants sagging a little already thinking I'm a college dropout or convict

Not guilty by affiliation but what society portrays me as

Because I'm wearing a black hoodie waiting to pay for gas,

Your equation is Black man plus black hoodie equals trouble

So the closer you get the tighter you hold your purse and kids

Now you standing close to me but know me from a far

But it's funny how your vibe changed once the cashier asks me for Identification and I pulled out my military I.D. card,

Now how does it feel knowing the same man you enslave with your judgment is the same man fighting for your freedom?

What do you see when you see me now?

Why do you let society views make you fear me?

Isn't that the reason so many young Black males been accidently killed by the police

So that means we should be judging all of you the same way you judge me

This is a true story...

HIV & AIDS IN THE COMMUNITY

Why does it seem people are too scared, dumb, or just ignorant to practice protected sex? We have been fighting the war against HIV & AIDS for years and have been losing for years. Our people struggle due to a lack of knowledge. Our culture is not informed on how many people are actually affected and ways you can become infected. If you would do your research and see the numbers for yourself, it would scare you to even kiss someone. There are new studies of STDs that are being founded daily. HIV and AIDS are all through the communities.

The scary part is that a lot of people don't know they even have it and is still living from day to day and having unprotected sex. But at the end when you start adding multiple medications to your daily life is when you will probably come to terms. But it may be too late. So please ask yourself are you trying to become the next victim. Remember it doesn't have a preference you can be Straight, Gay, Or Bi... Get tested...

According to the CDC an estimated 1.2 million people in the United States were living with HIV at the end of 2013, the most recent year for which this information is available. Of those people, about 13% or 1 in 8, did not know they were infected.

In 2015, 39,513 people were diagnosed with HIV. The annual number of new diagnoses declined by 9% from 2010 to 2014. African Americans are most affected by HIV. In 2015, African Americans made up only 13% of the US population but had 45% of all new HIV diagnoses.

Young people aged 13-24 are especially infected by HIV. In 2015, they comprised 16% of the US population but accounted for 22% of all new HIV diagnoses. All young people are not equally at risk, however. Young gay and bisexual men accounted for 84% of all new HIV diagnoses in people aged 13-24 in 2015, and young African American gay and bisexual men are even more severely affected.

In the United States, 6,721 people died from HIV and AIDS in 2014. HIV remains a significant cause of death for certain populations. In 2014, it was the 8th leading cause of death for those aged 25-34 and 9th for those aged 35-44.

HIV is largely an urban disease, with most cases occurring in metropolitan areas with 500,000 or more people. The South has the highest number of people living with HIV, but if population size is taken into account, the Northeast has the highest rate of people living with HIV.

Source: Centers for Disease Control and Prevention

Studies Shows That You Are Broke

Why do you continue to buy things you cannot afford then wonder how you got in that predicament? When the truth is you already knew what type of situation you were going to put yourself in, once you decided to try to keep up with other people who will get you broke or purchase something knowing you don't have the funds. Why put yourself in that situation to spend money you don't have. Learn how to invest, save, and have a retirement plan.

Stop living a rich life with a broke bank account and with a bankrupt mind frame. Too many jokes come with African Americans and bad credit. The sad part is a lot of those jokes are true. One more thing, Holidays and Birthdays are not meant to go broke over. Especially, when rent and child support is still due on the first. I believe that a child would rather have a roof over their head then a toy.

How are you planning to teach your child about being the master of money and not letting money becoming the master of your child?

Studies have found that 76 million Americans are struggling to make it or just making it barely. Studies also show that most people struggle due to not being financially educated or prepared.

What's Your Character Like

An act of kindness can go a long way. Some black people are always looking mad even when they have been blessed in abundance. Don't want to do anything for anyone unless there is something in return. Every time for years I would ride the metro and just look around. All I would see are angry faces. It takes so much energy to even keep your face looking angry. Some of you look like you practice in the mirror to master the angry look. Looking angry is not going to change anything. It's not going to change your situation or circumstance.

Then when you come in to contact with someone you want to be nasty and rude. This is one of the reasons why some of us walk with a chip on our shoulder because we continue to run into the same angry looking nasty people. But it can all change with one act of kindness. If we can spread rudeness we can also spread love. Sometimes an act of kindness can go a long way. Maybe if we start acting different amongst one another we may see change amongst one another.

Let's start by teaching our children what love truly is and how an act of kindness can go a long way. Anger will get them nowhere but in trouble and a lot of times they learn from home. Everything starts from home so remember that you can be the root of a blessing or the root of a problem.

Don't Let Your Dreams Die

They said the wealthiest place in the world is the grave yard. Because so many people with life changing & money making brilliant ideas were never put into action. Their dreams and goals along with their bodies went with them to the grave yard. Why are we so scared about what people think about us that sometimes forces us not to act on them?

The day we let what other people think about us determine our actions will be the day you let that person become the dictator of your life. Cut the strings and stop being someone's puppet. If you have a dream, goal, idea, or whatever; make it your business to make that into a reality. Stop side lining and get in the game. If not, you will just watch others make headlines and you will just continue to be the water boy even when you are better than the star player.

What's your insight on life...

Some people don't value life . . . They refuse to even evaluate their life. . They refuse to even give themselves a chance at life... Some people quit and believe their life is over. . . Some people never started living. . . Some people died before they learn to live. . . Some people believe that pain and tragedy are life. . . To some people money is life. . . Some people put a price on life. . .

Life can be Beautiful . . . Life can be Special. . . Life can be fulfilling... Life can be rewarding . . . Life can be adventurous. . . Life can be full of love. . . Life can be a Vacation. . . Life can be a Blessing. . . Life can be an eye opener to something Great . . . Life can be your Reason. . . Life can be your Purpose. . . Life can be all yours. . . Life is priceless. . . .

The Truth Is Life Is What You Make It . . . . Learn To Live. . . I Challenge You Not To Die. . .

Taking Responsibility for Self

Learn how to take responsibility for your own actions. We call ourselves grown but still play childish games. If you decide to cheat on your wife or husband and they left and you lost everything. The only person you can blame is yourself. If you did not reach a certain level in your life do not blame anyone else but yourself.

Why? Because 9 out of 10 times you did not give it your all or was too lazy and depended on others to carry you to your dreams or goal. No one owes you anything and no one can live or walk for you. McDonald's didn't make you fat, Your alarm clock didn't make you late for work, the MAN is not holding you down, Your child did not make you a dead beat father, Bills did not make you broke, Books did not make you ignorant, and Life did not make you a quitter. Take ownership and take charge.

Broken Signal

Cell phones have diluted the way we communicate with each other. We make cell phones our life, love, husband, wife, and anything that holds any significant value in our lives. Just look how families bond and watch how parents and children cannot put down their cell phones. Cell phones have become a distraction with family; communication, understanding, and moments amongst love ones.

Not the actual cell phone but the addiction of feeling that your cell phone is more important than what your child has to tell you about his or her day at school. More important than your spouse having something on their mind or they are having a bad day or just want to express how they feel. This is why so many homes are broken because the lack of communication. Put down the damn phones and pay attention to your family and friends. You are missing moments and hurting your relationship with your loved ones.

Distance Relatives

I been used and abuse by those who claim they Love me and I call family

But they're only family when favors or money are needed

Family is starting to not look familiar when unconditional Love is needed,

I keep them at a distance so they can't hurt me up close

But what do I do when I need family close,

I'm starting to become my own family

Because I can't trust my own family

This is why I can't wait to have my own family,

I'm a forest fire and the matches that started this blaze was grounded in my mother's purse

And wishing without thinking there's a motive

I too would like to be held close like my mother's purse

I always give but never receive

I been a grown man since the sandbox taking care of siblings like they were my seeds

When God blesses me with my Family I will treat them like Family and not distant relatives and they will unconditionally Love me

By the time the fool has learned the game,
the players have dispersed.
~Ashanti proverb

War has no eyes.

~ Swahili saying

This is becoming the Norm. . .The problem is this is not Normal. . .

The Famous Quote of The Streets. . .

WILLIAM LINCOLN

Gone To Soon

A DYING GENERATION

As we close 2016 I can't help but to think how many RIPs or Gone To Soon posts I seen on Instagram and Facebook. Or how many candle lights vigils or GoFundMe accounts that was shown on social media for those who have lost their lives to violence. The saddest part is that some people would say this is not normal for those outside looking in. But to those that live in poverty and street life their whole lives this is our norm. We should never have children or young adults that feel they will never see 18 or 21 because of all the deaths that surround them on a daily basis. So I ask you as a community. How do we save our youth from dying??? They are killing each other like it's the new fashion or trend.

The reality is before we blame this generation we must understand there were generations before this generation. So where does the blame actually start. How many young men and women were left for them to raise themselves??? How many was left stranded?? Rejected??? Motherless??? Or one of the most common effects Fatherless??? To really guide them to the right path and show them what path not to take because of their mother or father mistakes. How many children were given to the system against their own will???

Please understand that there is a reason. Rather it's a lack of guidance, love, and/or resources but us as a community need to step up and help this generation....

Social Entertainment

Social Media... Stop being entertainment for social media sites. We are becoming entertainment promoting ignorance and violence. How many times must we see people fighting, men beating a woman and think its ok to do so, children acting ignorant, cursing, twerking, and just continually showing the world that Black people are ignorant and don't care.

Imagine if you were a race that never had face to face contact with Blacks and all they had to go off was social media. I wonder what you would think of us.

Also, if you see someone in trouble or in need of help instead of recording it how about you lend a helping hand. If someone is being hurt and you are just recording it and they die and instead of calling for help or 911 and you just want to record the crime. You are just as guilty of their death as the person that is committing the crime.

Street Corner Options

Stop telling young people on the corner to stop selling drugs and not give them any options. Tell them why they shouldn't and then what they can do. Some of those brothers are trying to take care of their families. They are not going to stop just because you say so but they may if you give them options. Tell them about going back to school or jobs or anything. . .

Some don't want to be on the corner because of the risk factors. But when you have a child at home hungry, you are going to do any and everything in your ability for your family to eat. That's why it's so important to give them an option because some are not just doing it for their well-being but also for their family. So put yourself in their shoes. What would YOU do if your family was hungry, rent was due, and you were not receiving assistance? Give them a reason and an option. So instead of them being one minded to the matter they now have options.

Break Out OF Slavery Mentality

Slave mentality from social teaching running for my life. . . History taught us when slave master yells you ran . . . 400 years later different people but same mentality. . . So many years of getting abused by police officers now once we hear sirens we take off like a gun starting the race. . . Some of us be running for our lives and didn't do anything because we was programed to run when they tell us stop right there. . . Not understanding we are not always running because we are guilty but we don't want to be featured in the next YouTube clip… Stomping, punching, slamming, and beaten for no reason. . . This is the reason why you should know your law and know your rights.

WILLIAM LINCOLN

Tell Them Parent

Once I had you it was never about me

I may have to put my dreams to the side so your dreams can come alive

But that's fine because I want your life better than mines

Make sure you have the finest things even though I'm wearing the same ole things

Because once I had you it was never about me

Working hard like a slave so you can live like royalty

I spend more days working than at home tired and in pain cannot even come close to how I feel

Because once I had you it was not about me

Directing with Emotions

You should never make decisions off of emotions. Sometimes your emotions can blind you from using your common sense. From my own personal experience, make sure you take your time and let the smoke clear before making any drastic decisions. If not, you can put yourself into a situation that was quick to get in but a difficult process to get out. Sometimes we just want the hurt to go but we must stand through the storm before we make another storm on our own. Better said than done but try praying your way through a situation. Trust me it will save you time, energy, and money.

Explore or Stand still

Teach your children that the world is bigger than the hood. It wasn't till I joined the military that I stopped thinking that way. During my first couple of years in the Military I still lived in the hood because I felt safe. I became a product of my environment. So teach your child there are more places they can live other than the hood... That will enable them to explore life. That's why some people never left the hood and some of us will go visit and see the same people doing the same thing.

Bad friends will prevent you from having good friends.
~ Gabon proverb

Learning expands great souls.

~ Namibian proverb

In the moment of crisis,

the wise build bridges and the foolish build dams

~Nigerian proverbs

Show me your friend and I will

show you your character

~African Proverb

These Words Were Passed Down, Learned, Or Lived... I Pray You Find Them Helpful...

True Story

I have a good job, college degree, healthy, served in the military, educated, and enjoying life.

But my greatest strength is that I been homeless, locked up, broke, had my first child at 17, hurt by loved ones, lived in the hood and projects, and more...

Why? Because there is nothing else that can hurt me... I felt pain so I know how to deal with it. While some emotionally and mentally die from it because they never been through anything...

An elder person gave me insight about the riches of being Black. It gave me a new eye sight of my culture and how Beautiful we are...

Dirt is black...

Yes it is but the richness of the soil helps everything on earth grow...

Oil is Black...

Yes it is and yet you have Presidents willing to go to war over it...

Death is Black...

Yes which means we are the gateway to your maker and when you see the light which is bright as the sun think of us...

Stop Being Cheap

Support Our Youth

INVEST IN YOUR PEOPLE

I'm not forcing you to force God in your life. . . I'm just asking in your life let God come to life. . .

When Respect is received from the Respected it's when you know you are a game changer...

We can teach our youth on how to be free.

Freedom is not a physical state but a mental state.

Freedom is your choice. . .

Know the history of your culture…

Finding the truth of your culture is like finding the truth about yourself…

Lust can create confusion and illusion...

It will have you feeling and believing false promises...

WILLIAM LINCOLN

Your situation is not your reality

When You Are Ready To Go To War. . . Dress Like It. . . . In The Military They Have Uniforms. . .

Show Up In A Suit And Watch The Facial Expressions. . .

A Professional Black Man Is A Cultural Hero. . .

Judging people with no purpose can make you miss out on a Blessing. We judge from what we assume and not know.

It's sad how Black Businesses and Local Artists cannot get Support from their own People or City

WILLIAM LINCOLN

Today's music has our youth dying to say they are from the hood

When back in the days we was Dying to leave the hood

***

THE "N" WORD

It's funny how society portrays Young Black Americans but it's upsetting that sometimes we prove them correct which makes us rethink certain situations.

A DYING GENERATION

In the era of enslavement during the nineteenth century the word "Nigger" was a Black person's name given by a White person. Their original first and last name didn't matter much just the color of their skin. Nigger was the American name for a Black person. It was created as a degrading, derogatory, and disrespecting term for a Black person. While getting raped, killed, dragged, spit on, slapped, kicked, whipped, and so much more. That name was used over and over again. The verbal abuse went with the physical abuse.

Langston Hughes in The Big Sea (New York: Thunder's Mouth Press, 1940) stated about the matter:

Used rightly or wrongly, ironically or seriously, of necessity for the sake of realism, or impishly for the sake of comedy, it doesn't matter. Negroes do not like it in any book or play whatsoever, be the book or play ever so sympathetic in its treatment of the basic problems of the race. Even though the book or play is written by a Negro, they still do not like it. The word nigger, you see, sums up for us who are colored all the bitter years of insult and struggle in America.

In today's culture that word is the most common name used to describe Black people amongst each other. It's used in rap songs, comedy, TV, movies, and so on. Some say they don't care because it has nothing to do with their generation. Sadly, it does because somewhere down your bloodline your ancestors were killed, raped, and so on while being called that name. They fought so we can live a little better then how they lived.

Calling someone Bitch, Fuck boy, Pussy, Lame, or whatever cannot even come close to the word Nigger. That word created a system that you have now recreated that holds tears, death, family separation, embarrassment, and more within. I challenge you to do your research and find out the truth.

The N word was used to degrade Black slaves. It was used to degrade Blacks at the lowest level possible. It's worse than any word that you can think of. And as the people we did those a favor who still thinks we are worthless to carry on the name from generation to generation ourselves. We Recreated Our Own Nigga system.

WANNABE STREET NIGGA

A suburban young man wants to be a street nigga. . . Just because he thinks it's cool to talk about drugs and pulling triggers. . . Got some tattoos now he claims to rep that blood red or crypt blue even though his background is angel White . . . Claiming to be a general with no stripes. . . You are book smart but not street bright just because of the corner you stand at night. . . Pretenders like you are common but truly have no common sense. . . Cuz who in the hell would leave a home just to be on the streets. I rather be in my common house eating my common food in my common room thanking God for my common sense. . .

WILLIAM LINCOLN

I don't want my son to know what a Real Nigga is,

I want him to know what a Real Man is...

A DYING GENERATION

Nigga vs. Man

A real Nigga is a word that I only used when it came to doing something harmful or wrong. I'm a real nigga when I want to hurt someone or to prove my loyalty to something that wasn't in my best interest. Rather it had to do something with stealing, cheating, and etc. Having to holdup the reputation of a Real Nigga I had to continuously prove myself over and over. Do you ever hear of someone saying I take care of my child because I'm a real man or real nigga? Do you ever hear I have taken care of my family because I'm a real nigga? I never heard anyone ever using the real nigga term after speaking of that nature.

A real Man doesn't have to prove anything to anyone. He handles his household and business to make sure everything is in order. A real man takes care of his family and does not worry about holding up his reputation for the hood. A real man has morals and values and won't do anything that may take him away from his family. A real nigga is a conscious placement that we use to do things that we really may not want to do for the sake of showing others who we can become.

WILLIAM LINCOLN

THOUGHTS ON TODAY PARENTHOOD

> Instruction in youth
>
> is like engraving
>
> in stone.
>
> Moroccan Proverb

The problem with 'textbooks' is that they have not been inspected by the Black community, before they are given to our children. Plus, we have fewer Black people as teachers and administrators. The text books must inspire young Black people to read and learn. This is possible by showing that Black people have always been involved in inventions, computers, math, medicine, science, and other technologies, and by actually showing their faces. Knowing that people like you, have risen above poverty and other circumstances beyond their control, will inspire young Black people to dream of greatness, because they know people just like them, became great. (Even presidential candidate, Ben Carson, grew up very poor and became one of the greatest brain surgeons in the world, even though he is a terrible politician).

William Lincoln Jr.

Real Story...

I had a baby at 17. Having a child at that age was devastating because I was still a boy. I was doing homework in one arm and holding my daughter in the other arm. But I understood that before I wanted to do grown man things I had to step into a grown man place. There were a lot of things I wanted to do but couldn't because it wasn't about me anymore. Now I'm not saying once you have a child your life is over... Absolutely not... I'm saying life will be more complex when having a child that wasn't planned especially when you are young. You can hardly take care of yourself and to bring a child in this world think about the obstacles you face now... There will be somethings you will have to put on hold. But it does not mean your life is over. You will have to fight a lot harder and want it a lot more. So before you lay down with her or before you lay down with him. Be sure that you are ready for a lifelong commitment because there are no breaks or timeout in parenthood...

Mothers & Father

Make sure that you show your child Love so they won't have to feel they must get it from someplace else. Without the love from a mother, a man is more likely to sleep with other women just to fill that void and not respect women. Fathers, a young girl is more likely to sleep with men just to fill that void or put herself in an abusive relationship and actually think that it's love. Parents you are the first example of what love truly is. You must show your child what love is before society teaches them the meaning of Love. Some of us already been there and know that finding love in the wrong place can lead to a dangerous and dark road.

Television Raising Children

You too busy for your child so

Just put the TV on and let the TV watch your child,

You are tired and want to be left alone so to not have to deal with your child

Just put the TV on and let the TV watch your child,

When you want to talk on the phone and not be bothered

Just put the TV on and let the TV watch your child,

When you have a special someone to come over because you need sexual healing

Just put the TV on and let the TV watch your child,

You just want your child out of your way

Just put the TV on and let the TV watch your child,

But when your child becomes older and doesn't listen to you because he is in front of the TV remember who has been watching him all these years. So he is just returning the favor and watching the TV back.

Help Train the Mindset of Your Child

It seems that we are too busy to raise our children, so we let the television feed them knowledge. Depending on what they are looking at this could be a crucial moment in their lives. No books or family talks just cartoons playing over and over in the minds. There is no balance to help create a healthy mind frame.

Motor skills and social skills are reflected by what their minds are being feed. I wonder do parents actually look at what they are allowing their children to watch because they are too busy or they don't want to be bothered. You might want to take another look because there are some shows that come with messages that you may not want your child to comprehend. Don't let the TV raise your child that's your job. Don't be mad if your daughter's dream is to become a reality thot or your son wants to become a commercial thug.

Children are the new parents…

Children are raising other children because there are some females who do not want to be Mothers and men that do not want to be Fathers. There are so many children that have the worries of an adult because they must become the adult and the adult becomes the child because they feel they don't or are not aware of the responsibility of bringing a child into this world. Rather momma is too drugged to take care of the baby or daddy is to drunk now big brother or sister must take care of their baby brother or sister. We see it all the time in our communities. No child should have to be an adult to soon. But yet we have the nerve to ask what's wrong with this generation. There was a generation before this one. We let them down so we need to be asking what's wrong with us…

WILLIAM LINCOLN

Lost Child

Your child is no longer your child

Your child belongs to the government because your child is now a foster care child,

All because you picked drugs over your kids and the way of life beat you down emotionally you took it out on them and beat them down physically

Physically- you in handcuffs watching police take your kids away

Hurting the ones that depends on you to protect them and take the pain away

Drugs and heavy drinking gives you a new temporary life till shortly after you forever die and be the reason why everything you love be taken away

You staying in your condition but your kids are leaving

You help give life but you don't know if today will be your last day breathing,

Your life is broken and you need to get it together so you and your kids can be together

While kids ask how or why you would pick drugs over me

But you choose something that can't love you back

So picking drugs over your kids that God blessed you with instead of embracing that gift with a hug you just turned your back.

Dialogue

Government: Welcome

Child: Are you my new father

Government: No but let me introduce you to your new mother

New Mother: Hello… My name is System and I will be taking care of you……

Raising a Child

It takes a village to raise a child. Don't let your responsibility go to waste as a Grandmother, Grandfather, Aunt, Uncle, or Cousin. Come together to help your family continue to grow and prosper. Everyone plays an important part in every family member's life. Through our experiences, over comings, wisdom, faults, regrets, and knowledge about life and love, we have so much to give a child. Let's come together instead of acting like strangers and not continue to be distant amongst one another. Create a bond and not a space amongst one another. Help raise the future generation for your family so your family beliefs and values will forever live on. The worst thing you can ever do is avoid your responsibility to that child.

One of the most vital facts when becoming a parent is that once your child is born it's no longer about you. It's about your child. . . Selfishness is not an option. . . Give love, affection, guidance, and more. . .

Claim your child with authority and love... Never let them go and show them the way before someone else does...

A family tie is like a tree,

it can bend but it cannot break.

~ African proverb

If relatives help each other,

what evil can hurt them.

~ African proverb

Children are the reward of life.

~ African proverb

What you help a child to love

can be more important than what

you help him to learn.

~African Proverbs

It takes a village
to raise a child.
~ African proverb

***

A MESSAGE FOR THE QUEENS

She is beautiful; she has love, understand;

she respects herself and others;

everyone likes, loves and honors her;

she is a goddess.

African Proverb

Black Is Beautiful

Beautiful with History of Royalt

Beautiful with purpose

Beautiful with reasons

Beautiful with uniqueness

Beautiful with quality

Beautiful enough to still give you a warm smile even when your attitude is cold

Black Is Beautiful Beautiful to be Strong and Firm and will correct your ass if need too

Beautiful to be Loyal to stand by your side through the good and the bad times

Beautiful to Lift you up when you are down

Beautiful to Shine light in your darkest time

Beautiful to hold my composure till the right time Beautiful to be Bold enough to stand for righteousness…

Black Is Beautiful

Beautiful to be classy

Beautiful to enlighten

Beautiful to express emotions with a gracious touch

Beautiful to be a Blessing

Beautiful to be a Blessing to others…

Black Is Beautiful

Beautiful History of Strength

Beautiful to Birth Kings and Queens

Beautiful Minds & Thinking & Creations

Beautiful with No Expiration

Beautiful Soul

Beautiful Heart…

Black Is Beautiful

Beautiful is Me

Beautiful is You

Beautiful is Us

Beautiful Is Black…

This matter affects any race, age, and gender. Many that have experienced this are right under your nose. Your friends and or family members may have been closed lipped out of fear. Fearing you would judge them harshly for dealing with a man or woman that abused them instead of helping them plan a safe way out. It's not easy to share; I myself was in an abusive marriage. As a victim of domestic violence I lost my voice. I became silent and numb. I had forgotten how to live. Being victimized tears down your character, integrity, and self-worth; I spent many days looking within to figure out why this was happening to me. . . Why me? How could he? I thought he loved me! Constant questions that remained unanswered.

Domestic violence isn't just physical. It takes an emotional toll on the victim as well. . . I lost sight of my passion and dreams. Allowing numbness and fear to be the driver, I had become a trapped passenger. My Husband began as a loving man that I thought cared for me very much. In the beginning I was his pride and joy. He spoke high of me to others, and to the guys he would boast about my physique. Loving the feeling of belonging was wonderful. In the beginning the simplicity of life for us was good. He began to slowly change and I could not pinpoint the cause. Doing all that a wife could do didn't seem to be enough. The fights began verbally. At times there was no true reason to fight but he would start acting furious out of the blue and I would get the tongue lashes as if I had done something. He was a big guy with a loud and intimidating voice so naturally I was afraid of the possibilities. The verbal arguments grew into home possessions being damaged and/ or broken. After a while the verbal became physical. During the times of abuse, although no true reason was needed to spark his flame he had been caught cheating with other women and boy did I pay for finding out; Once the temptations of his job came into our home the abuse became often. My kids witnessed there father almost take me from them. As a mother that is a tough space to be in.

The optimistic family oriented side of me wanted nothing more than for the kids to have both parents under the same roof. I thought that was healthy for them. I was tired, and then I had become tired of being tired. How was I going to get out before I was taken out? Being tired I was still afraid of what would happen if I had tried to leave. My fear was huge. In my subconscious mind I thought "I had to stay because if I left I would strip my kids of having what I thought was the perfect picture of a whole family. The truth was that picture was broken in many places. Although I had learned to mask my pain and fears I was always crying out for help but no one could hear me. Afraid, lonely, and numb I had become a married woman that was married to a cheating single abuser. After many years of being a punching bag, being lied to and deceived, verbally abused and stripped of my character and self-worth I had enough. I found my inner strength and push to live for my kids and myself. The darkness was becoming light again. Having three beautiful children that I didn't want to see me weak and defenseless caused me to build a wall of tolerance. My kids deserved a true example of a strong Black woman. I was done with feeling weak and lifeless. I know the plan for life was greater than what I had endured. I had begun to find my voice. In mid-2013 I had enough! It was time to get out and I did. With no escape plan I had started to stand up for myself even if it meant that I could get hurt. Luckily I got out without death being the end result.

My children have shared with me in recent times a few things they recall from that dark period. Truthfully it was toxic and harmful. Children see and hear more than we give them credit for.

Shashika Washington

Chamar Logan is a mother, mentor, and educator. She is the editor in chief of the Women By Choice blog and relationship and motivational writer. Chamar's writing can be found on WomenByChoice.com and the Life's Diary Blog on Wordpress and Facebook. You can also find her writing available on her Instagram page

Email: chamarlogan@icloud.com

Instagram: @chamarlatanja

Twitter: @chamarlatanja

Periscope: Chamarlatanja

Snapchat: Chamar Logan

Dear Sisters,

As I sit here writing to you looking down on freshly manicured hands in the comfort of my brownstone apartment in Connecticut, I look out of the window with a cup of coffee in my hands and realize that I am extremely blessed. Though I know that I have come a long way and I yet still have more to go, I understand that the blessings I have now, with writing opportunities, speaking engagements, editor in chief of a national blog to empower women as well as the opportunity to build women, did not come from luck alone but came through hard work, perseverance, faith, prayer . . . and some very hard lessons. There are many things in my life that I am thankful for. There are many trials, testimonies and moments of perseverance that have made me the woman that I am today. A woman who is confident, secure, loves herself and is beginning to walk in the purpose that God has for her, a woman who is just starting to taste success. However, a lot of those lessons were lessons that came from poor decisions and not necessarily something I needed to go through. Life throws us enough curveballs that we don't ask for, the last thing we need to do is add more. I have often been asked the question "If you could write a letter to your younger self what would you say?" Those days are long past for me, but you are right at the beginning of your journey. We have a responsibility to pass lessons down to the next generation and impart wisdom and knowledge. You are the future, our hope, our dreams, and the next set of leaders. Every success I gain, every beautiful word or compliment spoken to and of me is nothing if you are not a reflection of that, young queens! Here is my letter to you.

One of my favorite Latin phrases is Nosce te ipsum "Know thyself" and one of my favorite Shakespearean quotes reads as such "To thine own self be true and it must follow, as the night the day, though canst not then be false to any man". These two quotes work in tandem with each other and is the basis for every life decision you will ever make. My beautiful young queens it is imperative that you know yourself. Self-discovery is the most vital journey you will make in your life and you will make it often. When you know who you are unequivocally you are less apt to make decisions that are harmful and not beneficial to you. Why is that?

Because when you know yourself you love yourself and you are less willing to bring anything into your life that is harmful.

I want you to understand that the process of knowing yourself will mean that you must let go of all desires to fit in with the crowd. It is easy to take on the identity of a group in an effort to do what they are doing and feel the false security of acceptance. This is often the first mistake in a series of harmful mistakes. God created you to be unique and special. You dear sister were never created to fit in and follow the masses. The definition of unique is being the only one of its kind; unlike anything else. When you read that definition you should see yourself reflected back. Growing up comes with its own set of challenges and pressures; these are easier to navigate if you know who you are and what you stand for sooner rather than later.

The next quote referenced refers to being true to yourself and not being false to any man. Once you know who you are, life will begin to test your values and your decisions. Never waiver from who you are, never waiver from what is right, and never do anything that is harmful to you, simply because it pleases another! Peer pressure goes hand in hand with this, your peers will pressure you to do and try things that are harmful to you mentally, spiritually and physically, you must have the wherewithal to say no and mean it. I have lost myself in many different ways because I gave away precious pieces of who I was to people that did not mean me well. These decisions of mine came with abusive relationships, alcohol abuse, mild drug use, suicidal attempts, and a near rape situation. I am thirty four years old and I didn't become stable in myself as a woman until I was thirty two. Those are a lot of years to build up pain, insecurities, and self-hatred all because I didn't take the time to know myself, know my worth and be true to who I was. Had God not stepped in and put me through a period of isolation in which I reconnected back to who he created me to be and what I was created to do, I would not be writing this letter to you. These days I have learned the importance of boundaries, I have learned that I cannot help other people if I am a mess, which means that it is imperative that I take care of myself and never do anything or make any decision that does not sit well with my spirit and who I am.

This is not an easy road and is often around less

traveled dear sisters, this is why it is important to surround yourself with positive like-minded people. Find a sisterhood of genuine support, honesty, love and success and hold dear to that. This may be only two or three but as Christ said "Where two or three are gathered together in my name I am in the midst of them".

Life is hard and beautiful. Life is full of challenges yet also rewarding. No matter what, your life is a gift, never waste it and cherish every moment even the toughest battles. You are royalty! You are more than conquerors and you are called to a greater purpose and a destiny that is unique to you. Know yourself, love yourself, know your worth, remain educated, and always reach higher. This above all to thine own self is true.

With love,

Your sister forever and always

Chamar

Marriage, a beautiful union of two people who are in love, It is a bond that holds so much promise. To be equally yoked, in sickness and in health, until death due you part. What no one tells you about this union is that you will learn so much about yourself. You will learn tolerance, patience and the value of honesty, compromise and communication. As a wife, you will submit to your spouse as he should to you. Not in the sense of one dominating the other but in the sense of working together.

I failed at marriage. It took some years to understand my place as a wife and make corrections. It was also difficult when you are the only one putting forth an honest effort. I saw the warning signs and chose to ignore them . . . The multiple women, the late nights, the condoms in the car. I understood "that men will be men" and I needed him . . . Because he said so, I also didn't want to fail and look foolish in the eyes of my family and friends. No one knew the struggles . . . The pain that I endured . . . So I left. After 10 years of marriage, I packed up my child and moved out of a 6,000 square foot house into a little 1,200 square foot apartment. I was miserable without him but I was determined to be successful because he put every stumbling block possible in my way.

I made mistakes, I did things wrong in my marriage. We disrespected one another, we fought, I said things that I should not have and there are no excuses. I said all of this to say. . . I'd marry again but I'd do things differently. I would not argue, fuss nor fight. I would take the time to listen and hear what he says. I would allow him to lead instead of always being the leader. We would always be a cohesive unit with God at the center of it all. Our love and union would be unbreakable as I have learned to be tolerant, patient, slow to anger and quick to listen. I understand what it means to be a submissive partner. I also understand that things don't matter but love and growth is KEY. Always be encouraged even in the midst of a storm. If it is worth the fight don't give up. Find a happy place even if you have to start over and work on you. I did. I still have some rough days but I am here and at peace with myself. Marriage can be a beautiful thing…

Esperita Garrison

A DYING GENERATION

It was invisible,

But she carried its blueness in her eyes,

Brushed it into her yellow strands of hair,

Smoothed it into her pale skin,

Subtly people react to the growth,

They don't know what it is but I know.

Do you want some, the smirk pinned

To the corner of her mouth, asked me.

I don't reply, just let my black hole eyes

Suck hundreds of years of that growing

Prejudice and crush it beyond existence.

I kiss my bronzed shoulders while letting out a scream as my reply,

The only Validation I need resides inside

My bones. . .

@phi.nitewords

She is Wifey-N-Training

Single because she don't want a title without the benefits

Highly educated in life and business but smart of enough to educate herself on how to be a wife…

She understands that her walk must match her talk and her action must match her heart

Daddy's little girl will blossom to became a wife but even roses can be deadly with thorns on the side. Thorns equivalent to baggage.

She works on herself while clipping each thorn off so when the day come she will board the married life with no luggage and fly so high they will honeymoon on cloud nine…

She is a Wifey-N-Training

She learns to cook with love so she can feed a man's soul

Stroke his ego and be humble enough to give him the keys so he can run the show

She is preparing for a type of life that is only fit for a wife

Tag team partner still holding her business down but will never put her man down but step to her man wrong she is willing to throw down, Rather a limo or a bus she will ride with you

She will be your umbrella during bad weather

Leaving her footsteps in your memories and becoming part of her history till your last breathe while she gives you a couple of forever…

She is Wifey-N-Training

What do you say when a woman tells you:

I'm with you not just start and finish but also in between

Because I understand I'm a queen because I'm with a king,

Look up at me and stop looking down

You may not see it yet but I see your crown,

Just never stop believing

I'm willing to walk with you in this journey til my feet start bleeding,

Even with a broken heart I will love you whole heartedly

I sacrifice my single life to live this life

I'm no longer in training I'm your actual Wife

WILLIAM LINCOLN

Reporting for duty My King...

A DYING GENERATION

Know Your Value Beautiful

Young Black Ladies, value yourselves as you are worth something. Why allow yourself to be degraded on a constant basis? Why not realize that you are Beautiful Queens that are living a false life that was given by society. You are living in a lie, an illusion that is keeping you from the truth that you are every bit deserving on what this world has to offer as anyone else.

You are fruitful with blessings and hold the true meaning of love as a Wife, Mother, and a Woman. That gentle touch can move mountains and heal broken hearts. You are a Queen of Royalty...

Once you understand your worth then you will understand your value. From there you won't tolerate Bull or put yourself in certain types of situations. Why? Because a Queen of Royalty does not deal with the Jokers that are there to just entertain her.

Why you mad if I call you....

If you always called yourself Beautiful-

Then I would call you Beautiful

If you always called yourself a Queen-

Then I would call you a Queen

But instead I always hear you call yourself a four legged animal that gets penetrated by other dogs

And continue to degrade yourself and refuse to upgrade yourself higher than what society graded you

Please tell me if I'm wrong

Rather you are a Bad Bitch, Real Bitch, Bomb Bitch, Hood or Rich Bitch at the end you refer to Bitch as your name,

So why get mad when I do the same...

Taking a Manhood Away

Women this is a very important topic. There is a difference between being independent and trying to be dominant. If you have a man and you continue to try to dominate him as the leader of the household please understand that you are taking away the meaning of his existence. The best quote I ever heard was that Women wants Love and Men wants Respect. Do you know that as being his spouse or significant other you only can take away what makes a man superior? For those who continue to throw how much more they make than their man or may take advantage of their man's kindness. Some may use children or threatening to leave to always have their way that will make a man feel belittle. Be careful while doing so because you alone could be breaking down your man. Please remember that a man is human and if you continue to speak down and continue to belittle him, and then you alone will and can break his spirit and the meaning to his life. . .

As much as I love people, everyone just can't go where I am going. So, I had to disconnect myself from some people and leave them as only a memory. And guess what? I AM PERFECTLY FINE WITH THAT! The problem is that too many people are trying to bring everyone along for the ride. We are who we surround ourselves with. Think about it.

Jacqueline D. Daniels

Learn to Love God

Then Learn to Love Yourself

Then You Will Know How to Love Me....

We play the lottery only when the jackpot is big. When it's small we don't want it. Sort of what we do when we praise God. When He's been good to us and opens doors we could not see. We praise Him when things are going good and kind of lose sight when things are going bad. But God says if we praise Him about the little things. If we praise Him when the bills are due. If we praise Him when we have no money in our pocket. He will reward us. He will supply all of our needs. He will give you more. We have to see Him in everything.

                     Jameelah Richardson

- I will say it for him because somewhere a man is thinking about this containing to you……

Better Than Me

I hope he is a better man than me

Treat you like Royalty and throw rose petals towards your feet

I treated my Queen like a peasant and gave her peasant time and peasant affection

You would get on the bus with me and you were OK as long as you were with me

Your thoughts were we could grow together and be better

My thoughts were on other things and I lost you

You deserve Happiness and Not Pain

You deserve Truth and Not Lies

You deserve Action and Not Excuses

I HAVE SEEN THE ERRORS OF MY WAYS

You are a Queen and I PRAY your NEW man is a Better man than ME

9-1-7

I will be your shield and take shots of hot iron lead smoking through my flesh with words carved pain, rejection, and failure. They said in order for you to live, something must die within you. We die together to become better. Just stand behind me as I make a path. Red tears from your past flowing out my pours. . .

I'm not asking for you to pull the trigger

I'm just asking you to hand me the clip

Holding you in my arms reflecting on past relationships that still in the present seems to have some control of your life

Well I'm Ready. . . Aim. . . Firing

Shooting down any negative thoughts while I'm encouraging why you would make the perfect wife. . . Reload

I'm not asking for you to pull the trigger

I'm just asking you to hand me the clip

You can have pin numbers and passcode.. Tag team. . . side by side. . . Even your shadow won't be walking alone. . . I will fight the devil for your joy and for you to breathe easy I will sacrifice my last breathe.

I'm not asking for you to pull the trigger

I'm just asking you to hand me the clip

Daddy issue- Shot down Family Rejection- Shot down

Broken hearted- Shot down

A man saying you could never do anything with your life and will never become somebody's wife

That thought gets a head shot- Blahh

Body bag those thoughts and replace them with new ones

If I call myself King and choose you to be beside me that

make you a Queen. But you were a queen before you even met me because you are the King of all Kings Daughter so you were born in royalty. You will have a life full of abundance and become a great wife. And if any other thoughts or feelings dare get in the way. . .

WILLIAM LINCOLN

Well. . .

I'm not asking for you to pull the trigger

I'm just asking you to hand me the clip

A DYING GENERATION

Right Man

You urging for a Black man but a Black man is not urging for you

So then you urge for a White man but a White man is not urging for you

Now desperate you put your morals to a side and leave your self behind just to have someone beside you

Maybe they see the God in you so God won't let them inside you because they have devil motives

But you do have free will and he will let you choose at your leisure

Just to be hooked up, lifted up, to be let down and now you want to forget it all

You praying for amnesia

If you knew your value, you wouldn't be selling yourself for discounted prices

You asked for a Black man

White man

Any man

WILLIAM LINCOLN

But not the RIGHT man

Be Patient Before You Get The Wrong Man

Unconditional Love is not judgmental…

Genuine Love Is When Your Man Feels Comfortable Crying In Front of You When He Is At His Darkest Time or Proudest Moment…

She's A Rare Woman

Women like her don't seem real anymore

God created them but man made them into something else because of their selfish ways and absent presence...

She's A Rare Woman

They call them thots, hoes, bitches, ghetto, and lost even though they are Queens

But the way this woman walks, smiles, dress, and acts she's not stuck up but will not conform to society because she knows she is Royalty...

She's A Rare Woman

Her sexiness is her class that can show a grown woman what a real woman looks like

Her sexiness is her class that can show a grown woman what a real woman act likes

Her sexiness is her class that can show any men she is worth more than a one night

She's A Rare Woman

She's A Real Woman

She Is A Woman...

Breaking Friend Zone

Maybe because you hold my word to my action and pinpoint when I'm slipping and raise a red flag when you see me bull-ishing

"Why is it so hard to be your friend?"

Maybe cause I say certain gestures as if I was your man but say I'm not serious, just for us to laugh it off but inside I'm really serious.

Because the woman who you reflect makes me reflect of my dream woman who I married and raise a king or queen because you already had it in your mind that you are royalty

"Why is it so hard to be your friend?"

Maybe because you hold me to a certain standard and demand and not ask that I perform like a grown man and will check a man to check if he's a man when giving off too many female tendencies

"Why is it so hard to be your friend?"

Maybe because you are one of the last females I know that will ride with me til the wheels falls off . . .Bang with me til the cops come. . . Cook & Clean . . . Heal me when I'm hurting and pray for me when my soul burning. . .

Maybe that's why

WILLIAM LINCOLN

Because maybe I want more than friendship...

QUESTION.... HOW MUCH DO YOU LOVE YOURSELF?

DO YOU LOVE YOURSELF ENOUGH NOT TO LET ANY MEN TREAT YOU ANY TYPE OF WAY

DO YOU LOVE YOURSELF ENOUGH NOT TO HARM YOURSELF OR PUT YOURSELF IN HARMS WAY?

DO YOU LOVE YOURSELF ENOUGH TO HAVE RESPECT FOR YOUR BODY?

DO YOU LOVE YOURSELF ENOUGH TO HAVE OTHERS RESPECT YOUR BODY?

DO YOU LOVE YOURSELF ENOUGH TO LIVE?

DO YOU LOVE YOURSELF ENOUGH TO LET THE OLD YOU DIE SO THE NEW YOU CAN EMBRACE LIFE?

DO YOU LOVE YOURSELF ENOUGH TO GO BACK TO SCHOOL?

DO YOU LOVE YOURSELF ENOUGH TO NOT BE A SIDE CHICK?

DO YOU LOVE YOURSELF ENOUGH TO DATE TO GET MARRIED?

DO YOU LOVE YOURSELF ENOUGH TO EMBRACE YOUR INSECURITIES?

DO YOU LOVE YOURSELF ENOUGH TO BE COMFORTABLE IN YOUR OWN SKIN?

HOW MUCH DO YOU REALLY LOVE YOURSELF?

Please excuse the Language...

But I found this very interesting because I always hear women say, "Love me for who I am..." But how can I love you for you if you do not even love you... Your physical flaw maybe my physical attraction... Just as stretch marks are Beauty marks to me. You gave birth and there's nothing more Beautiful than that. How can you expect me to love you for you if you are painting this illusion of someone else? You can still get naked without taking your clothes off by being secure in your insecurities... All I'm saying is that I should be able to recognize you in the morning without the additions. Stop caring and Live...

Ladies when you have a good man and he is trying to do better. . .

Don't hinder his growth or he will revert to his past. . .

I Need Attention

Yes I'm a man but I need attention too and please know just as much as you need me I need you too

I'm not asking for all your time or half the time just sometime and I'm fine

Cause while I'm helping you with your storm I may be going through mines so once we finish with yours

And to be able to be there for me like I was with you I would need you to pay attention to me too

I don't want to say anything cause I don't want you to think I'm weak I'm still that man that will go out and battle the world to make sure our family eats

My pride is affecting my emotions that I'm really not trying to express

I promise to continue to make sure your needs and wants are fulfilled

In exchange I'm not asking all the time or half the time but sometime give me my time and I'm fine

If you find "Miss This Year" beautiful, then you'll find "Miss Next Year" even more so.

~Nigerian Proverb

A woman who pursues a man for sex loses her spiritual beauty.

~African Proverbs

Milk and honey have different colors, but they share the same house peacefully.

~African Proverbs

You are beautiful because
of your possessions.
~Baguirmi Proverb

There is no beauty but the beauty of action.
~Moroccan Proverb

Patience is the mother
of a beautiful child.
~Bantu Proverb

Greatness and beauty do not belong to the gods alone.
~Nigerian Proverb

A woman's polite devotion is her greatest beauty.
~African Proverb

***

WILLIAM LINCOLN

A MESSAGE FOR THE KINGS

He who is destined for power does not have to fight for it.

~ Ugandan proverb

We are Kings and Leaders of our World. We lead our family into victory during despair and controversy. We are strong enough to take on the world and not just overcome but change perspective on the image of a Black man. We provide our family with unconditional love without being judgmental. We provide wisdom and share our struggles and regrets so our youth may learn from our mistakes. We show no signs of being tired or hurt. Even on our painful days we still smile because we don't let emotions conflict with our children's smile.

We teach our young and become role models and heroes to our sons and daughters. We treat our women like Queens and love our Wives like our lives depend on it. We praise God in public as well as in private so our children will know he is no secret. We are the structure and God is the foundation. Your wives make up the comfort of the home with her Love that you embrace.

We are not Niggas, Niggas was the word that slave masters used to name their slaves. That they feel wasn't worth nothing and held no value. We are Kings that have morals and values. We are the Light because we help make life and can help end life by deciding what we are doing with our life. So if you value your life then you will value the Light inside you.

William X. Lincoln 3rd

Black men must be the father figure for his sons and daughters and the loving head of the household and teacher of God's ways. For a Black man, I have always expected to keep my family safe and happy. Providing a nice home, good food, and a good education, along with teaching self-defense, and having income generating skills, is essential. Today, it is also necessary to know the laws, and get involved in the making of these laws by politicians, because these laws have always been detrimental to Black people. All fathers should give their children the benefits of his/her experience, so that the same mistakes do not have to be carried from one generation to another. Black men should also make sure that his family can be self-sufficient in many areas, like planting a food garden, mending clothing, and making repairs to the home and cars.

William Lincoln Jr. (My Father)

You holding yourself back

Always trying to keep the Black man down which could be true but I ask you. Who is truly stopping you from achieving what you want. I do believe that there are systems in place to keep down the African American race but it's up to us as a whole to let that happen. We must educate ourselves and stop giving so many excuses. Those who made it help your brother or sister out of the barrel. Don't just leave and not give back, start a domino effect so others will know how to. The day we stop being selfish, will be the day we will come together.

I miss the men that didn't dress up

Like women for some likes.

I miss the men that valued their

Masculinity- their God- given roles as

Men, Providers, Protectors, and Leaders &Builders

#BringBackOurMen

Leslie Christina

IG: @THEKINGSDAUGHTER_

Fortheloveoftheking.weebly.com

Be You Son

Men stand firm in who you are. Do not let any woman rape you of your self-confident or self-respect. We have too many situations where good men are having self-doubt not because of themselves but because of the opinion of their significant other. No man should be scared to be a man in the presence of his love one. Real love does not harm one another. If you do well by your family, Stand Tall. Demand your respect by talking to your significant other about how you feel and how she makes you feel. If your talk matches your walk then your respect should be matching all. Seek counseling or any support group that will help if you still feel you are not getting the respect you deserve because it could be deeper than you. But if you take care of your family, then you deserve your respect. Women wants Love and Men wants Respect.

WILLIAM LINCOLN

Sons of the Soil

The soil of the Earth is rich and life sustaining. It gives promise to tomorrow and beyond. When we left the land our fathers walked we were uprooted from the soil of our native land. We have bared scares and misery. Suffered, torment and abuse and still we stand rich in knowledge and character and strength. The soil has been tainted over and over yet in resilience we continue to move forward. Hold not unto the moment my young brothers for this dark and cold period in time shall pass. Our rich and life giving spirit will churn as the seasons that come and go, but in the end my brothers remember the soil must be nourished and cared for to continue to provide the richness of life.

Dean Smith 2015

When it comes to making money you cannot be greedy because that will make enemies and always look out for those who have potential in looking out for you in the long run. By doing this you will never have to worry about asking your enemy for a favor.

Michael Williams

Father

One of the most Beautiful gifts God has ever gave me was the ability to become a father. Men must not take this subject lightly as well as all parents. This generation is smarter than we think and know. Reach your children before someone else does. Communicate with your children and please understand that there is no more sugar coating the truth. Tell them about life and your regrets.

Give them a chance to hear from you and not from other classmates or people who want to just guide them in the wrong path. Be honest and they will thank you and understand. Some of these children have seen more than us in a short period of time. They probably know more about today's society than what you think. Do not sleep on them or they will wake you up in an urgent matter.

A father is the first line of defensive of showing a young girl what type of man to marry and a young boy what type of man to become. Take full advantage of that opportunity because we don't want our children to learn from the wrong person. . . TALK TO YOUR KIDS. . .

A Woman Reflection

Sometimes a woman can see her reflection from all the tears she cried. So ask yourself if you are part of that reflection. Are you part of her growth or part of her setback? As a man are you holding your queen down or are tearing her apart? You are rather going to add or subtract from her life. Can you honestly say you are pulling your weight or is she pulling both of you up the hill? Are you truly performing to the best of your ability or just staying content of your situation? How can you watch your lady turn into a Queen and just continue to watch yourself in the mirror not fulling your destiny as a King?

The problems that arise in your life only arrived because at some point you invited them over for drinks. So be mindful who you're surrounding yourself with, it is not better to keep your enemies closer.

Stacey Black

When you still say I in a relationship, you are still an individual. It's all about "We, "Us" and Together.

Chris Coward

Pride can tear a man down and hurt his emotion and he will be dying inside. Communication is key but understanding is what opens the door. We are so angry inside because we keep everything bottle up. If you are upset, then say you are upset. If you are mad, then say you are mad. If you are hurt, then say you are hurt. But you must stop keeping things locked inside and not letting those emotions out. You are like a walking volcano and everyone around you knows it. Stop being prideful and talk to someone so they can help you and you can help yourself.

Pride is like a disease that will kill you slowly inside if you don't have it treated. Talk to your pastor, father, brother, friend, counselor, or someone that you trust will be honest and genuine. Free yourself from yourself. . .

Lock up

Being in jail doesn't mean you are not free. You have one of the most precious things God ever created... Time... You have time to think about your life... You have time to consider your future, reflect on your past, and make changes in your present time. You can read and make plans to implement once you return home. You can change your own reality. Self-educate yourself so you will know how to achieve what you wish for in Life. Don't give up and don't stop believing. Don't let others feed you lies of no hope. That just means they gave up and want someone to follow them so they won't go alone. You are the King of Your Jungle.... The Captain of Your Own Ship... The Key to Your Own Lock . . . Only You Can Control, Guide, and Free Yourself from your circumstance. . .

A man is a provider

He provides Faith- To keep God closer

He provides Love- To his family

He provides Understanding- When you are misunderstood

He provides Communication- When things need to be clarified

He provides Security- To show he is not leaving

He provides Protection- Protect his love one's heart

He provides Confidence- When you are insecure

He provides Courage- When you are scared to try

He provides Compassion- To wipe your tears

He provides Companion- To walk with You

He provides Prayer- Even when you are too tired to pray for yourself. . .

Choices

It's not easy to always do the right thing. But as men we must understand that we are leading the next generation of men. How we speak, act, live, believe, and treat others starts with us. We learn from our recent generation and upbringing. Now the next generation will be learning from us. It's very important to understand that you will be starting a cycle. Now what you will be passing on will be up to you. Rather we can continue to pass down the wrong message that will continue to cripple our culture or we can pass down knowledge that will help them succeed in life. The choice is yours. . .

Let's Talk

Let's talk about somethings that were told to us about what makes a real man. I have been through it all and as I realize that there was somethings that we followed while growing up that actually crippled how we live today. We were always told that men don't cry. They say that crying releases the pain from the soul. Now I'm not talking about always crying and rolling all over the floor. What I'm saying is when that hurt is overwhelming or pain is overwhelming we need to release it. Shed those tears so you won't unleash it on a love one. If your son is hurt as a father, uncle, cousin, or friend it's our job to comfort them. Let them know it is okay before that angers boils and explode.

No snitching is a concept that cripples our neighborhoods. We were taught that you shouldn't snitch so the person that may have killed or robbed someone was set free by the community. So those who were running free in the neighborhoods committing crimes enslaved the community. That's why people feel they must watch their backs to even check the mail or go to the corner store.

We cannot always depend on law enforcement to

care about our communities as much as us. It never hits home until it hits home. Then we want to make sure the police find the same person you didn't want to snitch on. Protect your community and take back control of it.

Situations

Something simple as sitting in a seat while a woman is standing beside you and not asking if she would like to sit down can set us back generations. Why? Because you never know who is watching. Of course we are always being watched. It allows the woman or women depending on how many are watching upgrade their thoughts about Black men. Let's be honest a lot of them already think we are not worth a pot to piss in. We can't be too mad because we gave them that belief.

Also you never know when a young boy is looking and notice your actions and decides to follow your actions. You just reached another generation. Now he decides to follow your steps not knowing that's not how a Real Man conducts himself especially if he doesn't have a male figure in his life to show him the correct way to live.

So imagine if that's only one person with one situation. Imagine the whole culture with every situation you can think of.

A DYING GENERATION

Black Man Ingredient

God Is Inside A Black Man

Royalty Is Inside A Black Man

Greatness Is Inside A Black Man

Strength Is Inside A Black Man

Leadership Is Inside A Black Man

Faith Is Inside A Black Man

Favor Is Inside A Black Man

Courage Is Inside A Black Man

Loyalty Is Inside A Black Man

Gifted Is Inside A Black Man

Honor Is Inside A Black Man

Commitment Is Inside A Black Man

Vision Is Inside A Black Man

Goals Is Inside A Black Man

Determination Is Inside A Black Man

Overcoming Is Inside A Black Man

VICTORY IS INSIDE A BLACK MAN BUT. . .

It's up to you to bring it out. . .

He who thinks he is leading and has no one following him is only taking a walk.

~ Malawian proverb

If you are filled with pride, then you will have no room for wisdom.

~ African proverb

When a king has good counselors,

his reign is peaceful.

~Ashanti proverb

A happy man marries the girl he loves,

but a happier man loves the girl he marries.

~ African proverb

To get lost is to learn the way.

~ African proverb

There can be no peace without understanding.
~Senegalese proverb

When there is peace in the country,

the chief does not carry a shield.

~Ugandan proverb

The wise create proverbs for fools to learn,

not to repeat.

~ African proverb

***

WILLIAM LINCOLN

Reflections Of The Past

A DYING GENERATION

I DREAM A WORLD

I dream a world where man

No other man will scorn,

Where love will bless the earth

And peace its paths adorn.

I dream a world where all

Will know sweet freedom's way,

Where greed no longer saps the soul

Nor avarice blights our day.

A world I dream where black or white,

Whatever race you be,

Will share the bounties of the earth

And every man is free,

Where wretchedness will hang its head

And joy, like a pearl,

Attends the needs of all mankind--

Of such I dream, my world!

Langston Hughes

WILLIAM LINCOLN

When A Man Angers You,
He Conquers You.
Toni Morrison

FIND THE GOOD.

IT'S ALL AROUND YOU.

FIND IT, SHOWCASE IT AND YOU'LL START

BELIEVING IN IT.

JESSE OWENS

WILLIAM LINCOLN

THERE IS NEVER TIME

IN THE FUTURE IN WHICH

WE WILL WORK OUT

OUR SALVATION.

THE CHALLENGE IS IN

THE MOMENT, THE TIME IS ALWAYS NOW.

JAMES BALDWIN

IGNORANCE, ARROGANCE, AND RACISM HAVE BLOOMED AS SUPERIOR KNOWLEDGE IN ALL TOO MANY UNIVERSITIES.
ALICE WALKER

I WON'T HAVE ANY MONEY
TO LEAVE BEHIND.
I WON'T HAVE THE FINE
AND LUXURIOUS THINGS OF
LIFE TO LEAVE BEHIND.
BUT I JUST WANT TO LEAVE
A COMMITTED LIFE BEHIND.
MARTIN LUTHER KING, JR.

IN ORDER TO HAVE A CONVERSATION WITH SOMEONE, YOU MUST REVEAL YOURSELF.
JAME BALDWIN

HE WHO IS NOT COURAGEOUS ENOUGH TO TAKE RISKS WILL ACCOMPLISH NOTHING IN LIFE.
MUHAMMAD ALI

I'M BLACK.

I DON'T FEEL BURDENED

BY IT AND I DON'T THINK

IT'S A HUGE RESPONSIBILITY.

IT'S PART OF WHO I AM.

IT DOES NOT DEFINE ME.

OPRAH WINFREY

> YOU CAN'T JUST SIT THERE
> AND WAIT FOR PEOPLE
> TO GIVE YOU THAT GOLDEN
> DREAM, YOU'VE GOT TO GET
> OUT THERE AND MAKE IT
> HAPPEN FOR YOURSELF
>
> DIANA ROSS

I TRY TO DO THE RIGHT
THING AT THE RIGHT TIME
THEY MAY JUST BE
LITTLE THINGS, BUT
USUALLY THEY MAKE
THE DIFFERENCE BETWEEN
WINNING AND LOSING.
KAREEM ABDUL JABBAR

WE ARE NOT

MAKERS OF HISTORY.

WE ARE

MADE BY HISTORY.

MARTIN LUTHER KING, JR

WILLIAM LINCOLN

FEW ARE TOO YOUNG,
AND NONE TOO OLD,
TO MAKE THE ATTEMPT TO LEARN.
BOOKER T. WASHINGTON

HOW FAR YOU GO IN LIFE
DEPENDS ON YOUR BEING
TENDER WITH THE YOUNG,
COMPASSIONATE WITH THE
AGED, SYMPATHETIC WITH
THE STRIVING, AND
TOLERANT OF THE WEAK AND
STRONG. BECAUSE SOMEDAY IN
LIFE YOU WILL HAVE BEEN ALL OF THESE
GEORGE WASHINGTON CARVER

YOU ARE THE PRODUCT
OF THE LOVE AND AFFECTION
OF YOUR PARENTS, AND
THROUGHOUT YOUR LIFE
YOU HAVE DRAWN
STRENGTH AND HOPE FROM
THAT LOVE AND SECURITY.
NELSON MANDELA

THERE IS NOTHING
ESSENTIALLY WRONG
WITH POWER.
THE PROBLEM IS
AMERICAN POWER IS
UNEQUALLY DISTRIBUTED
MARTIN LUTHER KING, JR.

WILLIAM LINCOLN

OF MY TWO "HANDICAPS,"
BEING FEMALE PUT
MANY MORE OBSTACLES
IN MY PATH THAN BEING BLACK.
SHIRLEY CHISHOLM

BUT FOR OURSELVES WHO KNOW OUR PHIGHT TOO WELL, THERE IS A NEED OF GREAT PATTERNS TO GUIDE US, GREAT LIVES... TO INSPIRE US, STRONG MEN AND WOMAN TO LIFT US UP AND GIVE US CONFINDENCE IN THE POWERS WE, TOO, POSSESS.
LANGSTON HUGHES

WILLIAM LINCOLN

EVERY INTERSECTION
IN THE ROAD OF LIE
IS AN OPPORTUNITY
TO MAKE A DECISION,
AND AT SOME TIME
TO ONLY LISTEN.
DUKE ELLINGTON

RACISM IS A CONTEMPT
FOR LIFE, AN ARROGANT
ASSERTION THAT ONE RACE
IS THE CENTER OF VALUE
AND OBJECT OF DEVOTION,
BEFORE WHICH OTHER RACES
MUST KNEEL IN SUBMISSION.
MARTIN LUTHER KING, JR

WILLIAM LINCOLN

RECOGNITION WILL DO
MORE TO CEMENT THE
FREINDSHIP OF RACES
THAN ANY OCCURRENCE
SINCE THE DAWN
OF FREEDOM.
BOOKER T. WASHINGTON

NATIONS, LIKE MEN,
ARE WARY OF TRUTH,
FOR TRUTH IS TOO OFTEN
NOT BEAUTIFUL.
ADDISON GAYLE, JR.

WILLIAM LINCOLN

BECAUSE TIME HAS BEEN
GOOD TO ME,
I TREAT IT WITH
GREAT RESPECT.
LENA HORNE

I BELIEVE IN HUMAN
RIGHTS FOR EVERYONE,
AND NONE OF US IS
QUALIFIED TO JUDGE
EACH OTHER AND THAT
NONE OF US
SHOULD THEREFORE
HAVE THAT AUTHORITY.
MALCOLM X

***

WILLIAM LINCOLN

Supporting Black Owned Businesses

***

NeeCee Simmons

@wifeyntraining

Shopwifeyntraining.com

Denise "NeeCee" Simmons, a Pittsburgh, Pennsylvania native holds a BS in sports management and a MSA in Organizational Management in Human Resources. However, NeeCee is no stranger to the entrepreneurial world. Raised by her father whom she cites as her hero, she watched him build his brand & grow his own business over the years without the benefits of advertising.

This key influence from her father is something that would later unknowingly turn pain from her life experiences into purpose, and passion into profit, by utilizing the 21st century's most powerful technology, social media.

In search of self-healing inspired by heartbreak, and self-esteem issues, NeeCee founded Wifey N Training™ a full service online resource page to Encourage, Build, and Prepare women for the triumphs and challenges they may face as it relates to personal relationships and dating.

Upon putting her vision out into the social media atmosphere, NeeCee organically grew over 200,000 Facebook fans as well as over 20,000 fans on Instagram.

"I suffered from low self-esteem and I've been lied too. I now know my job is to help encourage as many women as God allows during their journey to happiness, self-love, and more." (Denise "NeeCee" Simmons).

NeeCee Simmons

@wifeyntraining

Shopwifeyntraining.com

Wifey N Training™, under the NeeCee™ brand has grown to become the parent company for: Shop Wifey N Training, Hubby N Training™, WNT Book Club, and The Worth the Wait Empowerment Tour.

NeeCee has not only been able to empower women and men in the process of healing herself, she's also able to strategically show other small business owners or purpose pushers how to empower themselves to profit.

While the business aspect was an unexpected blessing for NeeCee, she is now positioned to take her vision to the next level globally.

NeeCee's current projects are included but not limited to: Ebooks, Empowerment Tours, Social Media Strategy Plan, and Global Expansions on both Wifey & Hubby N Training Projects.

In the future NeeCee also wants to tap into Magazines, Film Production, Radio and MORE!

***

Stacey Black

Born in Washington, DC and raised in Concord/Charlotte, NC with a gift to praise and worship. God placed Stacey Black on a path that seemed to some certain for destruction. If not from generational curses or physical ailments the mere fact of living in a single parent home in a contorted world already predicted chaos. But God had a greater plan though. Aligning true family, friends, and well-wishers around him, the growth in this now 32 year old recording artist is apparent. Servicing his lyrics as bait to draw in willing and unwilling vessels to Christ is what his main focus has become.

No longer focusing on self-centered advances in the world but homing in on spreading the gospel of Jesus Christ. Which is the direction he was giving at a young age through the leadership of Pastor and Uncle Royce L Woods and many other great men and woman of God throughout his life!

Over a span of 15 years this artist has recorded singles with Heartbeat Entertainment and International Hip Hop artist/writer J-ROD to create the R&B love ballad's "Baby Girl" (produced by Antonio Adams/John Woods) and "Number 1" (produced by Jody Jazz). Conjointly, a list of additional recordings, writings and arrangements can be accounted for as well.

After a time of growth, a decision was made and he signed with Christian Indie Label PULSE MUSIC GROUP in 2012. Under C.E.O and Co-Founder of PULSE MUSIC GROUP Antonio D.

Adams and Dora Adams in 2013 he released a compelling transparent EP project entitled "Changing Directions: The Murder of Me." A 7 track memoir of conviction, repentance and faith. Amidst collaborative writing and developing vocal ability to better minister to the world he is also emerging as an entertainment entrepreneur as C.E.O of Black Inc. Entertainment. A management firm structured around artist development and arranging kingdom class social events. Which purpose lays congruent to his music ministry.

Now in 2016, Stacey Black is looking to do greater with his forthcoming freshman album "ALEPH" while understanding greater, and expecting greater from GOD! Walking into the future praising and worshiping Christ all the more!

To know God, Christ and the Holy Spirit is a very delicate experience. it is a great and wonderful experience. It's like you begin to see that in you is something so great that wrapping your mind around it is impossible, but just to think on or accept the realness is awesome!!

www.reverbnation.com/staceyblack

A DYING GENERATION

www.pulsemusicgroup.bandcamp.com/album/changing-directions-the-murder-of-me

blackinkentcontact@gmail.com

***

WILLIAM LINCOLN

ONE OF THE BEST DJ'S IN THE WORLD

A DYING GENERATION

Jeremy "DJ Mix-I-Am" Reaves

Jeremy Reaves is a native Washingtonian, a professional musician, and DJ. He is also the owner and founder of HH Studios which is located in the heart of Washington, DC. Some of his musical accomplishments as a professional musician and DJ, consist of various Television Networks, Radios, and Public appearances, which include "The Titans Music Awards," "The Eddie Kane Show," and The Rock The Flow To The Couch Series."

He is a graduate of Winston-Salem State University where he obtained his Bachelor Degrees in Rehabilitation Studies. Mr. Reaves has been an active member of Phi Beta Sigma Fraternity Inc., an organization that prides itself on servicing the community with youth driven mentorship programs. His personal mission has been to inspire and educate the youth to walk into their own purpose and recognize their weaknesses as strengths.

Mr. Reaves continues to share his passion and love for God through his music and his voice by teaching others that they too, can achieve anything they set their minds to. His passion for Hip-Hop and Traditional Urban inspired music continues to feed his hunger in becoming one of the most influential entertainers in the game.

Contact Information:

Phone: (202) 215-0029

Email: jeremyereaves@yahoo.com

Website: www.mixiament.com

***

Dominic R Williams

Associate Consultant for Kingdom Builders Financial Consulting LLC

Chief Executive Officer and Co-Founder of Dynamic Multimedia Group DMG

Chief Operating Officer and Co-Founder of Longevity Investment Team L.I.T.

Chief Executive Officer and founder of Heavenly Hands Catering, Personal Chef and Hospitality Service

IG: MR_DYNAMIC_1

I started my first business at 22. Since that day entrepreneurship has been a way of life for me. The keys to success reside within your daily habits. You pay your bills with your 9-5 job, you establish wealth with your business you run from 5-9. I'd rather put in 80 hours a week towards my own business than to put in 40 hours for someone else's. If your dreams don't scare you, then you are not dreaming big enough. I focus more on my source (GOD) than on my resources. Always value people more than you value money.

Dominic Williams

Associate Consultant | Business Development Specialist

Kingdom Builders Financial Consulting LLC

301.785.5209

dominic@kbfinancialconsulting.com

www.kbfinancialconsulting.com

MICHAEL M. WILLIAMS

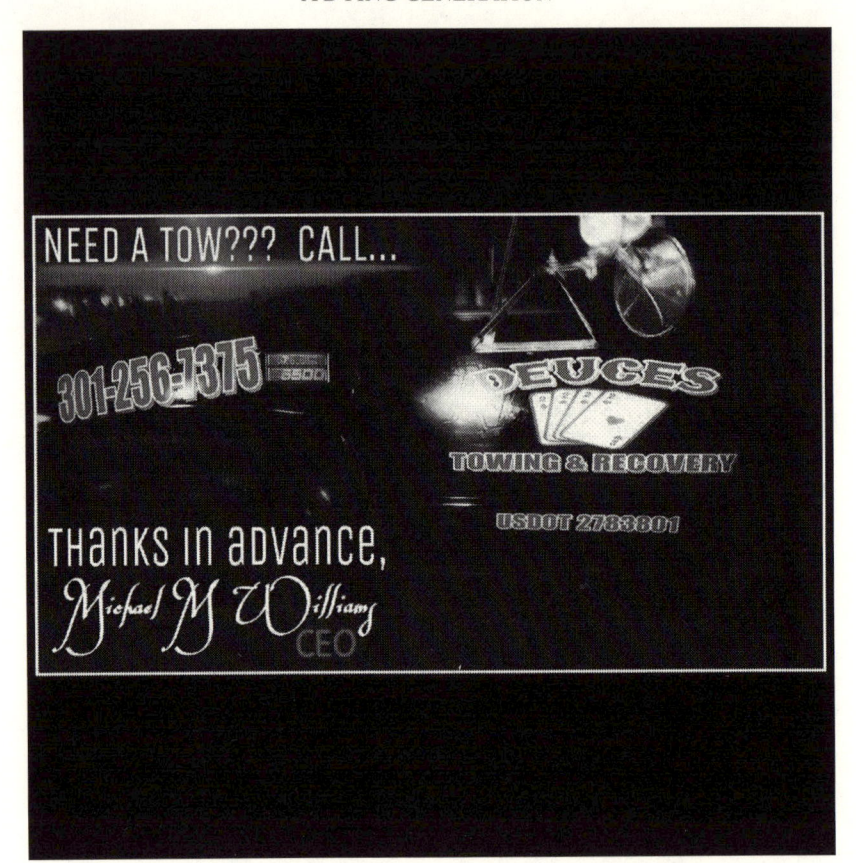

***

Veronica Pearson

Company Profile:

Dammi is a multi-platform media lifestyle company that encompasses film, PR, publishing and lifestyle brands. Dammi is an innovative and digitally progressive media company in North Carolina- the trusted voice informing, engaging and entertaining audiences and communities via film, prints, websites, radio stations, events and dynamic digital venues. Founded in 2005, Dammi has provided exclusive brand management, publishing, and film production to clients with advisory services in every aspect of development and operations related to brand building and film production. In 2015, Dammi added PR to its portfolio of brands. Dammi's PR branch has branded and hosted events for Values partnerships, OWN Belief series, Sony pictures and more. The firm specialized in global film production, brand marketing, content publishing and lifestyle brands from fashion to furniture.

Veronica Pearson Bio:

Veronica Pearson is one of media's game changers. Born and raised in Charleston, South Carolina, she grew up designing and writing. Joining the military to pay for college, Veronica traveled around the world studying design and learning about other cultures to enhance her brand. After spending years in Naples, Italy she decided to return to the US and start Dammi, a fashion house in Charlotte, NC. After major success, she took her earnings and developed her own global media company. She is an accomplished producer, director, and writer; from film to print. Veronica has received recognition within the industry, with her military short film "For Our Country", to her multiple celebrity produced PSA videos for the #rebrandblack campaign, which promotes positive narratives about Black culture in the media. Veronica resides in Charlotte with her family.

Veronica Pearson

dammiinc.com

***

A DYING GENERATION

FOTR
FUTURE OF THE RETRO

WILLIAM LINCOLN

FUTURE OF THE RETRO

A DYING GENERATION

Welcome to the Future of the Retro family!

We are not just another brand we are a movement. Everyone who supports FOTR has earned an elite place within this movement that is destined for greatness. The meaning of our name is something that is worth being brought back up in the future and maintains the same relevance regardless of society changes. For example, your favorite pair of Jordan's. . .your favorite old school song, something being so good that its ability to resurface and be relevant is almost impossible to be denied. Not only will our apparel fall into this category, but also the individuals who recognize the greatness within themselves to become the future leaders of the world. If we just described you, then you are Future of the Retro! Register here today to be eligible for discounts and receive our new release newsletter. Thank you for your support!

CHECK OUT www.futureoftheretro.com

***

Jamila Green

I stand for justice. I stand for peace. I stand for eliminating this sad corruption. I see myself as the Lady of Justice through my clothing line; thus the logo. My stand firm conviction for one day making a difference in the government & our society is personified through my clothing line. When you wear

Checks & Balances, you feel a sense of empowerment, self-confidence, and self-awareness.

As a stylist, I always seek to discover whatever my client's passions are and how they view their greatest inner selves to personify through their style. Fashion is skin deep! I'm excited to join Model Mayhem to connect with this vast network, and utilize my talents to further reach out my growing career.

checks_balances@ymail.com

FACEBOOK: CHECKS BALANCE

INSTAGRAM: CHECKSANBALANCES

***

Special Reynolds

Special Reynolds, age 23. Born and raised in NYC. I have always answered my calling for helping others. I volunteered in Honduras helping the children there with their studies and also involving them in numerous activities. When in cosmetology school,

I gathered together a couple of my friend's classmates and organized a event to do hair and makeup for those who couldn't afford it in preparation for the teen's prom.

I've recently joined the Uhuru movement, which helps bring African People together no matter where on the planet they are from. We give political education to our communities worldwide. Letting it be known that we are one! I am a licensed cosmetologist. For the future I would like to open a nonprofit salon for families and individuals who cannot afford it and also a Black owned supermarket.

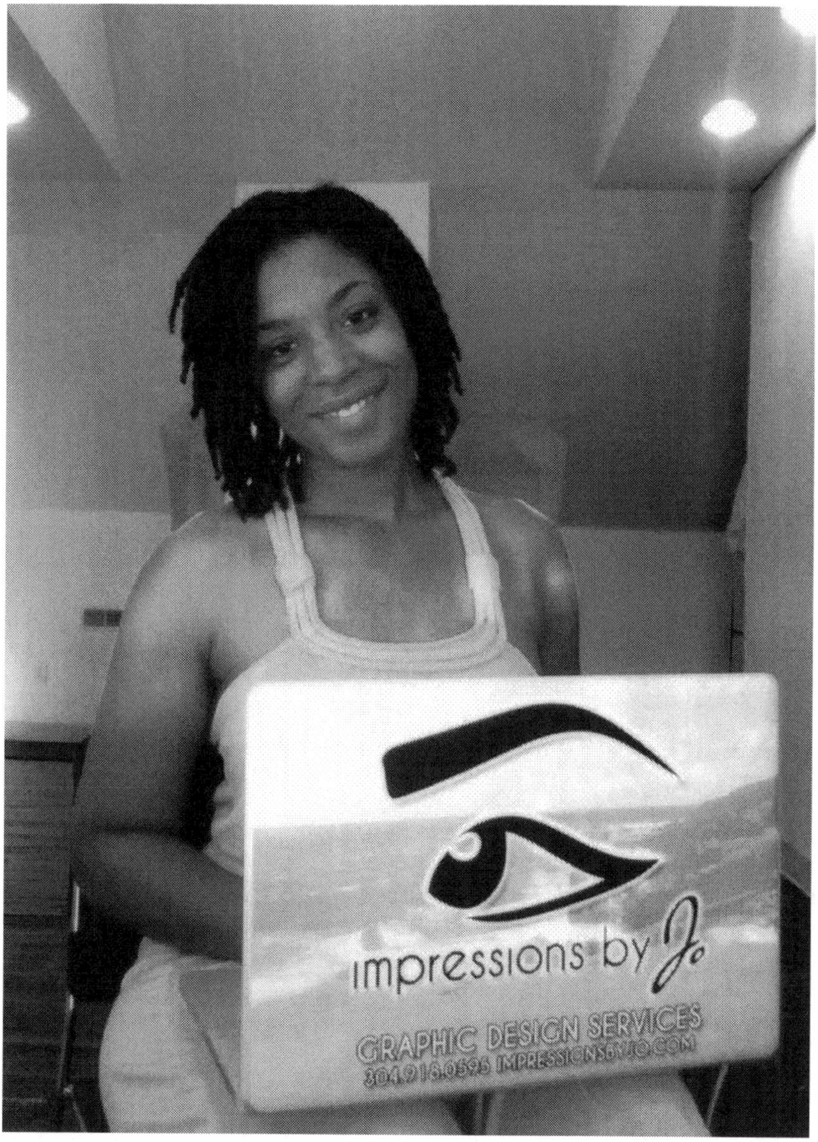
impressions by Jo
GRAPHIC DESIGN SERVICES

impressions by Jo
GRAPHIC/WEB DESIGN SERVICES

The human mind is an incredible thing. It can observe its surroundings and produce magnificent things.

We owe EVERYTHING to these stimuli, these catalysts that get the creative juices flowing. My intention with every project is to honor my muses by projecting the impression they left on me into captivating works of graphic design.

The most valuable inspiration is you, the client. *An impression by Jo will always be a reflection of you.*

Contact:

Website - www.impressionsbyjo.com

Instagram - @awakenintruth

Email - impressionsbyjo@gmail.com

***

A DYING GENERATION

Taji-maq

Taji is a Black Beauty & Culture quarterly specialty publication that embodies both the traditional and modern royalty of Pan-African people. We celebrate our culture and arts with features from our community across the globe. Our mission is to provide the Black community with positive images of Black Beauty, Fashion, and Family as well as highlight the positive efforts of those in our community and provide information on health and wealth specific to our needs.

Info@TajiMag.com

***

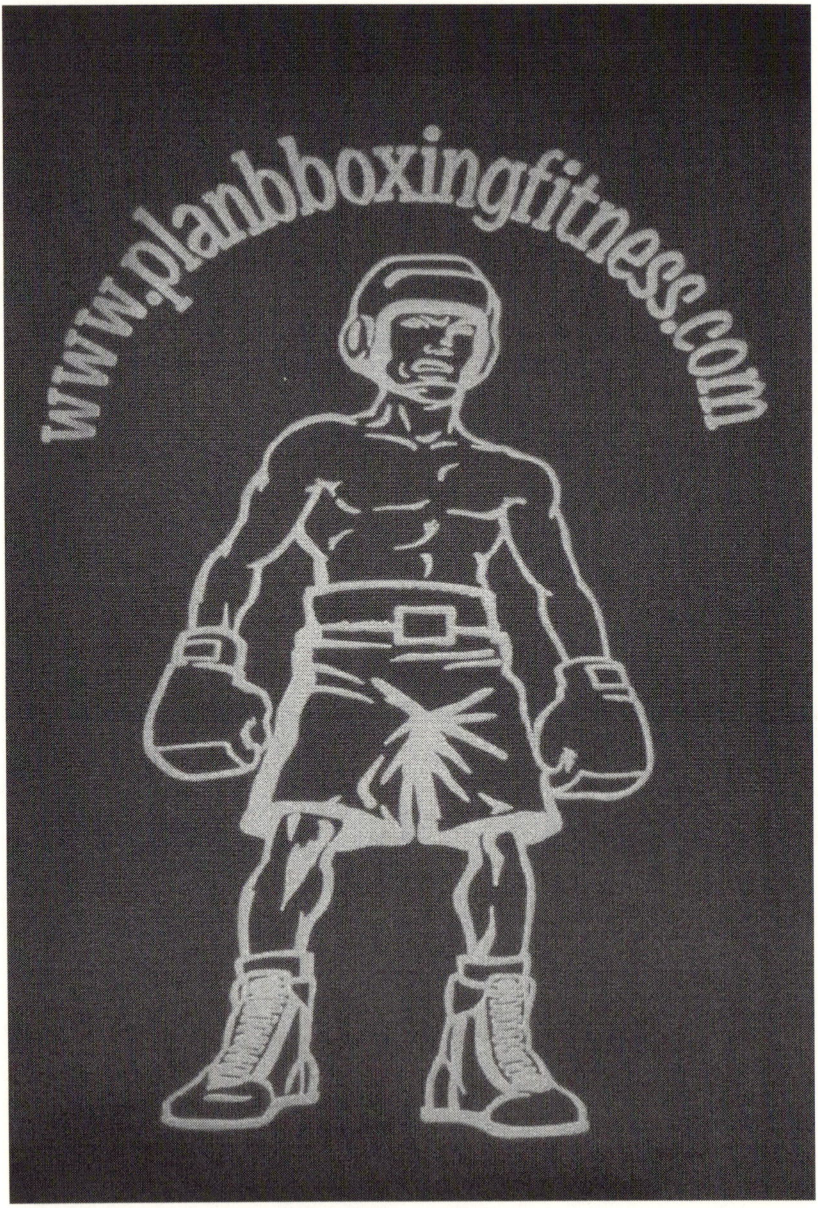
www.planbboxingfitness.com

Juan Samuel

Plan B Boxing Fitness LLC., we bring the gym to you anywhere in MD. We provide all boxing equipment, trainers & gas included in prices.

We offer professionally-influenced boxing & workouts for all levels (and ages), designed for those who expect to be pushed harder than what typical everyday gyms offer.

***

Melanin MADE
EST 1990

mel•a•nin

Melanin is the root that gives color to skin, hair, eyes, plants, oils, animals, landscapes

...

anything imagineable that is creative and colorful.

@MELANIN-MADE

My Name is Geylynn Scales also known as "Queen G". I was born in Saint Louis, raised in New Orleans and spent my teenage years in Kansas City Missouri. I have always been aware of our people and how we were not treated fairly but it hadn't become clearer until I moved out on my own in 2012 to attend college at University of Missouri St. Louis. In my time being there the Mike Brown case happened which forced me to see things how they really were. At the time I was in school for Graphic Design and my teacher wanted us to come together and to create designs to make more people aware of what was going on but it wasn't enough for me.

I ran into an old friend later that year and he introduced me to Hidden Colors and after watching those documentaries it all became clear. From then on it's been a mission to educate but in a way that the younger generation as well as those who are not knowledgeable can relate to. Why not do a clothing line where messages can be displayed and desirable. I came up with my first concept in November of last year and then the brand began to expand and take on its shape. Melanin Made name was chosen so it won't be constrained to doing just one thing and the color and design where inspired by modern

African patterns in clothing. Making it a modern design was essential in creating a brand that would stand out.

Melanin Made's purpose is to take modern images and visuals and merge them with concepts that elevate how we think of ourselves as a people. My goal is to get this going so we can contribute to other people and foundations that are in the business of advancing our people and our youth.

QUEEN G
CEO/DESIGNER
816.695.0715

MELANINMADE90@GMAIL.COM
MELANIN-MADE.COM

@melaninmade90   @melanin_made90

Melanin MADE

www.blacktongueclothing.bigcartel.com

Kipri Johnson, Owner

Black Tongue Clothing

BTC

Black Tongue Clothing was created to embrace Black LOVE, LIFE & CULTURE. Black Tongue Clothing creates wearable, thought provoking works of art that make you question your commitment to the survival of Black culture. All designs are original and exclusive to this brand. Black Tongue is my form of self-expression on the past, present and future state of Black America. Through this media, I expect patrons will initiate solution based dialog on the topics that affect our health, wealth and freedom.

www.blacktongueclothing.bigcartel.com

"America is false to the past, false to the present, and solemnly binds herself to be false to the future."

-Frederick Douglass

**

A DYING GENERATION

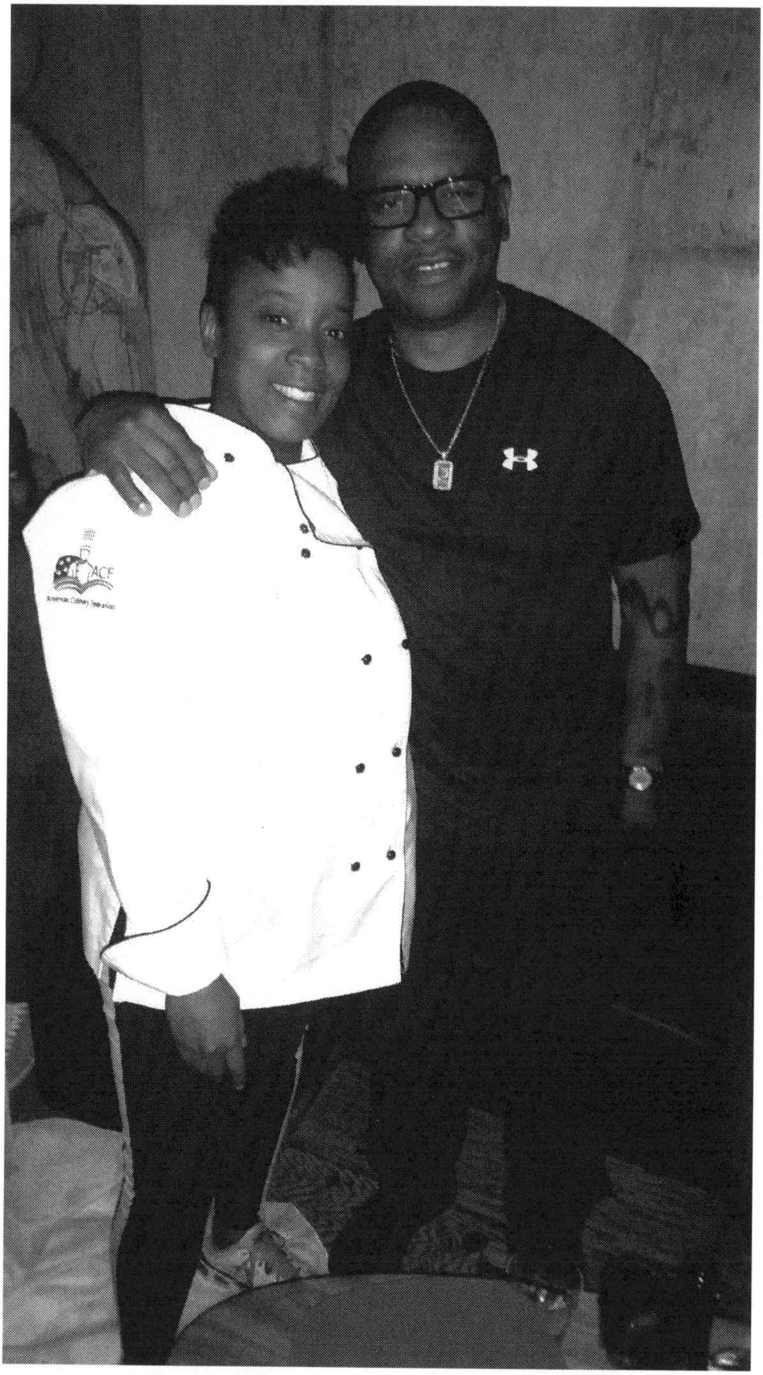

A DYING GENERATION

Andeidra G. Bell was born and raised in the inner city of Baltimore. From an early age she always had a passion for cooking. It came for her endless hours in the kitchen with her grandmother and mother preparing Sunday dinner. In 2005 with no formal training she decided to take her love and passion for culinary arts and open a catering company. That is how Tre'Chaz Catering Co was formed. Tre 'Chaz is your down home cooking specializing in southern cuisine. Her philosophy was that she wanted to bring back the days of family dinners. Her slogan "Treating you like family" and the concept was to bring back the days of family sit down dinners. The business was doing well but times took a turn for the worst. While pursuing her passion recession hit and caused her to put her dreams of having a large catering facility on hold. She still did small functions but not on the scale she once did. In 2007, she then decided to pursue a career in the medical field as a billing and coding specialist. After 5 years of doing that the passion for cooking still lingered in her mind. After a divorce in 2011, she decided that she needed an outlet to regroup and that when she decided to bake cupcakes for family, friends and small functions.

The rave reviews and constant request for her cupcakes gave her an idea. This is how Cupsey Cakesy By Dee was created. Cupsey Cakesy was a hobby turned business in a blink of an eye. Cupsey Cakesy is not your typical cupcakery they have a twist, they can turn any of your favorite "Cocktails" into a cupcake. While she was building her business she decided she wanted formal training, she has her degree in Advanced Culinary Arts and she is currently pursuing her degree in Pastry Arts. She is due to graduate in June 2015. Andeidra has more than 8 years of experience with catering, hospitality and baking.

cupseycakesy@yahoo.com

***

WILLIAM LINCOLN

A DYING GENERATION

WILLIAM LINCOLN

A DYING GENERATION

Jon Brick

Jon Brick (BrickArt) is a Baltimore based conceptual artist. Skilled in techniques including Acrylic painting, graffiti and graphic design. Jon Brick is a graduate of Bowie State University in which he graduated with a Bachelor in Fine Arts in 2007. Since then Jon Brick Art's can be found displayed in cafe's and galleries across Maryland. In addition to custom art work he also instructs painting sessions for people of all ages these sessions are more popularly known as "Sip and Paint" or Paint parties.

Contact info: (443)8451111 jon-brickart@gmail.com

Jon Brick of BrickArt

***

Arminta McKinney

I love God and I love spending time with my family and friends. I'm a single mom to my son Miles, who is the light of my life. Photography has been my passion since I was a child and in 2004 I launched my career as a professional photographer. While I cover several genres of photography including portraits and weddings, working with families and children is my absolute favorite to do. I love lazy days on the couch watching movies, however I'm a true busy body. I love to give back and I absolutely love to travel.

Arminta McKinney

My business is AM by Arminta and AMDLD Photography

I can be reached at armintacmckinney@gmail.com.

Dear God,

I come to you in praise and thanksgiving for all that you have and will do in the lives of our youth! I glorify you and am in amazement of every expectation and line of order that you have for their souls!

All the accomplishments, goals, admiration that through you they will reach!

Lord, your WORD says that greater is HE that's in me than he that is in the world!

So I know that with your power every strong hold can be brought to its knees and every chain can be broken.

Lord generational curses will be exposed and demolished by the Lord of Angel armies!
Lord, its inevitable that the "enemy" and "inner me" will try to stand against the vessels you've created

but when Christ left his comforter that let us know that everything, I mean Everything will be alright! My Great, Awesome, faithful Father I thank you for the concerned men and woman, Mothers and fathers, neighborhoods, and communities.
The ones that cry out to you and intercede for a

new and fresh anointing for the generations!
I praise you for the past generations that prayed and praised and were obedient to the call.

The call of loving others. The call to help others. The call to proclaim the name of Jesus Christ.

Now the blood of those fervent prayer flows to the new generation and they WILL do the same!

You are Great GOD and I proclaim that this generation will not die but LIVE for you!

Hallelujah and Amen

***

Made in the USA
Middletown, DE
13 July 2024

57257724R00184